LIPSHTICK

GWEN MACSAI

LIPSHTICK

Perennial
An Imprint of HarperCollins*Publishers*

For Ruby, Mo, and the next great expectation

A hardcover edition of this book was published in 2000 by HarperCollins Publishers.

HarperCollins books may be purchased for educational, business, or sales promotional use. For information please write: Special Markets Department, HarperCollins Publishers Inc., 10 East 53rd Street, New York, NY 10022.

First Perennial edition published 2001.

Designed by Lindgren/Fuller Design

The Library of Congress has catalogued the hardcover edition as follows:
Macsai, Gwen.
    Lipshtick / Gwen Macsai. — 1st ed.
      p. cm.
    ISBN 0-06-019101-5
    1. Women—Humor. I. Title.
  PN6231.W6M345 2000
  814'.54—dc21   99-24462

ISBN 0-06-093061-6 (pbk.)

01 02 03 04 05 ❖/RRD 10 9 8 7 6 5 4 3 2 1

CONTENTS

LIPSHTICK

PART I

THE BLUNDER YEARS

Laugh and the world laughs with you.
Cry and you cry with your girlfriends.
—LAURIE KUSLANSKY

A GIRL WOULD BE ONE LOST SOUL WITHOUT HER girlfriends. An astronaut severed from the mother ship, yin without yang, an Oreo without the middle. Girlfriends are the elevated, the wise, the Good Humor truck on a hot summer day. We are bonded together like protons and electrons — nothing short of a nuclear blast could split us apart. We are together, we are one, we are *sistahs*.

Your girlfriend is your priest, your sounding board, and your fashion consultant all in one. She is almighty and all for-giving. She will watch you drown in a gallon of Rocky Road and happily grab a spoon. In the harsh reality of the morning light, she'll know just where to take you shopping for clothes without seams. At 50 percent off, no less. She is your mother without the guilt, your sister without the competition, your therapist without the bill. She is sustenance itself, and without her life is a vast pool of emptiness.

I heard a story the other day that exemplifies this perfectly — everything there is to know about girls and girlfriends in one telling anecdote. It involves a man who was coaching his eight-year-old daughter's Little League team. His team was in the field when the batter hit a ground ball and it went right to the shortstop. She scooped it up, beaming with pride at her accomplishment. Then she promptly threw it to the center fielder.

After the game, the group went out for ice cream, and the coach did the unisex politically correct thing: He congratulated them all on playing so well, told them how great they were, and talked a lot about teamwork and how important it is. Then he pulled the shortstop aside and said, "That was a great pickup you made on that grounder, you did a terrific job, but I know that *you* know that the ball should have been thrown to the first baseman. So tell me, how come you threw it to the center fielder?"

The shortstop just looked at him incredulously and said, "She's my best friend."

And there you have it. Girlfriends rule.

The heart of a girl is a sweet and complex morass. There is no telling what lies there until you pull on your boots and clomp around for a while, pick in hand. Sometimes you have to hack away at it for years and sometimes things come gushing out in a torrent. And it is like having the winning lottery ticket to have a pass to a girl's heart and what lies within — a rare privilege indeed, for she invites in only those who have proved themselves worthy (by slaying a dragon, pulling a sword from a stone, or maybe just cleaning out the coffeepot once in a while like he's been asked time and time again).

I know that you are just that kind of a person. You have worthy written all over you. You are a pillar of worthiness, a human testament to worth (or, maybe I'm not so picky). And that is why I extend an invitation to you to trample away. My heart is your heart. Bring on your flashlight, your chisel, your TNT. It's a jungle in there. Think of me as your own personal cadaver to cut open and explore. Maybe you will learn something, or maybe you'll just puke your guts out.

The following pages are an open confessional — come right in, I say, plunk yourself down, get comfy, and let's chaw, tawk, kibbitz, confess.

I have chin hair.

There, I've said it. Now you know it. We can move on. You take a turn, then I'll take a turn, and when we are done, we'll be forever bound. Then you can see if what is close to your heart is close to the heart of the girl sitting next to you. I guarantee that it will be, and then you are on your way. The two of you have a beautiful future together. You can talk over the most minute event in excruciating detail over coffee. Or coffee cake. Or, since one of you is dieting, fresh fruit. And then the circle is complete. Girlfriends beget girlfriends and the world keeps turning. They are the ones who will be there for the psychological dysentery that can hit after you drink from the wellspring of life. You will never be wanting for an ear, a shoulder, or a safety pin. In the great baseball game of life, you'll be playing short-stop, and before you know it, you'll be fielding grounders.

A SNOWBALL'S CHANCE

Be careful of puppy love; it can lead to a dog's life.
—GLADIOLA MONTANA

TWELVE IS BIG. VERY BIG.
Mainly because it's almost thirteen. At the age of twelve, a
girl has to weather the worst storms, most of which start
brewing in the very abscess of psychological functioning:
junior high. You may as well throw a drowning girl a brick.
Divorce, bankruptcy, fear of death, these are fragrant flowers
in life's bouquet compared to junior high. It is a prepubescent no-man's-land. A weigh station. Something to do after
elementary school that bides your time until you set foot into
high school, where everything in your life that is ever going
to happen happens—you hope to God. It is a heady time.
Yeasty, in fact, when mounds of breasts start rising all over
the school, inviting unwanted attention from every zit-
studded moron walking down the hall. And the zit-studded
morons walking down the hall are wearing the same shirt for
weeks on end, still wildly entertained by imitating farting
noises. This preoccupation with fart sounds keeps every single boy from noticing that the girl with breasts the size of
Hershey's kisses is secretly following him home from school,
practicing her married name (his, of course) in the margins

of her notebook, and forcing the Ouija board to spell out his name at each and every slumber party.

It is the Sahara of self-esteem. I was a girl who had hair down to her waist, a face like stucco, and breasts that once inspired a lingerie saleswoman to growl, "Thirty-four A? Hah! You're a training bra if I've ever seen one!" And all I could think was: But what can you train them to do?

In junior high I lived for only one thing. Greg Alcoke. He was it. My destiny, my fate, my obsession. He: Sonny; me: Cher (only he didn't know it yet). Everything about him exuded cool: the way he let one strap of his overalls hang open when he walked down the halls, the way he parted his greasy hair right down the center, his fantastic I-don't-have-a-care-in-the-world saunter, and his mild irreverence when it came time to obey the rules and treat our misbegotten homeroom teacher with any kind of respect. It was a recipe for love.

When we spoke, a single tear of sweat would trickle down between my breasts in training.

Since he was in my homeroom, I tried on occasion to muster up the confidence to do more than just sneak a peek at him. Sneaking a peek was an exercise that entailed pretending to look straight ahead while forcing my eyeballs over to my right ear. On rare occasions, I ended up sitting next to him (we were part of an "open" classroom, no seating charts) when he came late and the seat next to me was the only one left. I would have liked to sit next to him more often, but such a bold move on my part would have been widely seen as a neon sign of my feelings, a brazen gesture, and it would have earned me voracious teasing that was sure to ruin my *real* chances with him. When these rare opportunities presented themselves, however—during attendance, for instance—I wanted desperately to come up with some witty repartee. Something Nick and Nora–ish. Unfortunately, all that I could put together was usually something like, "Do you have any extra vermiculite? I have to replant my mung beans."

My really big chance to be close to Greg, to touch him, to pretend that I was his girlfriend, came only once a year during gym, when all athletic endeavors stopped for a week, the bleachers were folded up, and we were forced to take *Social Dance*. It was universally feared by all the girls (in a titillating kind of way) and coolly scoffed at by all the boys. The good thing about it was that you didn't have to take showers and endure the taunts and stares of the eighth-grade toughs who wanted you to live in fear of them, which, of course, you already did. Compared to running the risk of getting their attention for the wrong reason, I was all too happy about Social Dance, when the worst that could happen to you was that you'd have to stand in the same gravitational field as a geeky guy with gray teeth and raw-onion-like B.O. oozing from every pore.

Back then, Social Dance was the only unit in gym that was co-ed. It corralled boys on one side of the gym and girls on the other like a hormonal high noon. At glacial speed the sexes met, sweaty palm joining sweaty palm in a pas de deux so awkward, the gym ceiling had never been more closely examined. While couples where swaying around the gym like so many arm-out zombies, Mr. Crane, the bulky, balding gym teacher forever in sweatpants and a cap that made him look like a refugee from Burger King, was stationed in the corner, pretending he was a late-night DJ. He caressed the microphone lovingly and closed his eyes as if he was envisioning himself onstage at Caesar's Palace instead of in a grotty gym where it was raining estrogen and testosterone. He didn't seem to care that the record player was an old AV dinosaur and that the 45s sounded like they were being spun under a Brillo pad. This was *his* turf, and he clearly fancied himself the Barry White of Nichols Middle School. He played only Motown, and for that alone, we loved him. In the middle of each song, he would call, "Snowball!"—a cue for everyone to change partners. Most, too embarrassed to expose their *true* love interest, would just turn to the nearest person and grunt in universal preteen code.

"Uhhhhhhh, yuwannadance?"

I knew where Greg Alcoke was at every moment. Usually in the arms of someone hipper, taller, and more developed than me. He danced with assuredness. His palms, I was sure, wouldn't be sweaty. If only I could get close enough to find out.

"*Snowbaaaaaal!*" Mr. Crane crooned as I tried to snowball my way over to Greg. But it didn't work. I kept getting snowballed by people who led me farther and farther away from my one true love. Then, with five minutes left, Mr. Crane raised the stakes. His voice boomed through the crackling speakers. "Last dance, take a chance. Find that special someone. Don't be shy, be a lover guy, use this dance to tell them they're *special*." And he put on the best, most romantic song ever written, "Let's Get It On." I looked around. The choices were dim. Then, out of nowhere, there he was! Greg Alcoke, right next to me!

"Uhhhhhhh, yuwannadance?" he asked in a bass voice that suddenly burped soprano. We danced. Lights, camera, action. It's a movie—a love story—and *I* am the star! Close up on his face, his shoulder. I love you, Marvin Gaye.

Then Greg did the meanest thing he could've possibly done. He moved to another state. One dance and he was Colorado bound. I was devastated. Heartbroken. I pined, but I forged ahead. I graduated eighth grade, went to high school, graduated, went to college, dropped out, went back, graduated (finally), and had (somewhat of) a life. And in that life, umpteen years after my last Snowball, I was ushering for a play at the Steppenwolf Theater in Chicago. It was a day not unlike any other one I'd ever lived. It was intermission and I was behind the candy counter selling bonbons. Someone asked for a box of Milk Duds. I looked up. It was Greg Alcoke! Right in front of me! The first time he'd been in town since junior high, and there we were—BOOM!

A single tear of sweat trickled down between my *finally* trained breasts.

"Greg?"

"Gwen?" His voice was reassuringly familiar.

"Oh my God!"

"You look exactly the same!"

"Don't remind me . . ."

"This is so *weird* . . ."

The monumentalness of this moment was not lost on me. I felt no obligation to pay any attention to the man Greg had come with, another junior-high classmate of ours. Not that I was purposely giving him the cold shoulder or anything, I mean Valentino himself could have been standing right next to me and I would have never known. And if people were asking for service at the candy counter, I didn't hear them. In fact, as we greeted each other, everyone else in the room just disappeared as I took a metaphorical step back to take a good look at Greg Alcoke. He looked good. Especially now that his hair was clean. Lean and tan, a little weathered. Okay, so he wasn't Sonny, but who was I, Cher? He was *Greg Alcoke.*

Enough said. I knew I was staring at him, but I couldn't help myself. What kind of cosmic spin had my world taken that Greg Alcoke was standing in front of me all of a sudden, out of nowhere, like an apparition in the flesh? What was the likelihood that this would ever happen again in my lifetime? My shock undid me. I felt something creeping up my gullet, about to spill out. Fortunately, it was only words.

"I was so in *love* with you in junior high!"

He was silent.

I got so warm, so fast, I felt on the verge of spontaneous combustion. His eyes nervously darted around like they were following the flight path of a wayward fly. Then he looked right at me with a kind of calm, with a little tiny smile that I will never forget. Almost like he was remembering a really good joke.

"I know," he said.

Far off in the distance I had a sense that the world was still moving, that life still existed, though I had no proof of it in the vacuum that was this moment. He knew. He *knew!* It was like I was in Social Dance all over again listening to Gladys Knight: *"Dreeeeaaams don't always come true, uh-uh, no sir,"* as if I needed a reminder. I prayed for it to rain hot lava. Nothing came.

"I know."

In my mind, the scene fades to black. I remember nothing more of that evening. "I know" closed the Greg Alcoke chapter of my life with a sonic thud. I never saw him again.

Finding the right boy to lust after is a lifelong struggle. Eventually, you grow to be picky about who rejects you. But at twelve, you can't help but hurl yourself at boys (if not physically, emotionally at least) like so much pasta at the wall, despite the obvious mismatch that will cause you to slither off said wall and fall into a limp heap on the floor. We all would have been saved a lot of time, misery, and obsessive behavior if someone had been so kind as to mention this to us back in junior high. Maybe a line or two in the tampon instruction booklet: "Unwrap, insert, and don't bother with the really cute boys since they will end up breaking your heart into a thousand pieces and eventually get much fatter than you anyway." Maybe your homeroom teacher could slip it in somewhere: "Okay, for tomorrow, chapters three and four of *Sounder,* and by the way, Tiffany, you are on the road to ruin when you pine after Brandon like that. Take a second look at Irving—that dandruff is surely temporary."

But it is hard to say how much success this would have yielded in an audience of seventh-grade girls who were busy worshiping at the feet of such icons as Davy Jones and David Cassidy. Besides, for people like me there are some humiliations you just have to live through repeatedly, for years on end, until you are close to death when the message finally starts seeping through.

And twelve? Twelve is just way at the beginning. *Way.*

CRUSHED

Can you imagine a world without men?
No crime and a lot of fat, happy women.
—NICOLE HOLLANDER

MEMORIES OF YOUNG adulthood aren't things that most people relish. In fact, I would have to venture a guess that in exchange for a guarantee of excising these memories from their cerebral cortex (along with the Captain and Tennille—to say nothing of Peaches and Herb), most people would gladly sever a limb or two. And, in fact, most people have, in effect, done just that. The memories may still exist, but they are so far back there, they are hanging around with Cro-Magnon man. These people don't remember a thing. Not a teacher, not a classmate, not a cafeteria tray full of shit on a shingle. Except, of course, me.

I remember everything. I mean, I couldn't tell you the year the Civil War started, the capital of South Dakota, or how you really spell "necessary," but I can tell you the name of every teacher I ever had, the combination to my fourth-grade locker—22–6–17—and who sat three rows up and two rows over from me that year—Leo Lindo, whose real name was Clinton. I run into people from my past constantly. It's like I have an unintentional radar that secretly guides me toward them. Though I love it, this is something my friends hate about me: I have actually been naked in a sauna without my glasses and have recognized the fleeting view of a woman walking past the glass door as someone I hadn't seen since the late sixties, when I was under the age of ten. Since this happens so often, I am no longer so stunned by it, but every once in a while, one of these unexpected reunions can send me reeling into a state of wild excitement, utter astonishment, and deep existential shock.

Such was the case of Lucy Kaplansky.

Lucy Kaplansky and I were in the same homeroom in second, third, fourth, fifth, and sixth grades (Ms. Study, Ms. Davis, Ms. Pliss, Ms. Niedenthal, and Mrs. Fano). She was one of the girls in my school whom you just wanted to be with, hang around, emulate, and, if you were smart, cheat off of. Anything in the hopes that a little bit of her very Lucyness might rub off on you. She was one of the smartest people in the class and *we* were buddies.

She was Lucy! She had a brother named Spike and a mother with raven-black hair. She chewed on her tongue while deep in concentration. She came to my house and I went to hers, even though we lived miles away from one another. At school we sang Oh-ho-the-Wells-Fargo-wagon-is-a-comin'-down-the-street in music class with Ms. Giesela Goetling, a woman who was easily nine feet tall with legs like mighty oaks. We studied fruit flies with Mr. Benson, wrote a play with Ms. Pliss, climbed ropes for Mr. Patlak, and together went to the all-girl assembly where Ms. Thigpen, the school nurse, told us everything there was to know about menstruation (information some of us wouldn't need for years. I was a late bloomer, and all of the you-are-about-to-become-a-woman hoopla surrounding the sacred ceremonial menses was in sharp contrast to the, shall we say, unspectacular actual event. This proved to be a foreshadowing experience. Numerous future lessons in life and love took on that same basic pattern: intense anticipation paired with demoralizing letdowns—all culminating in a little brown shmutz). But after sixth grade, I moved. We lost touch. Twenty-two years went by. And ten life-times later I was working as an associate producer at National Public Radio when one day I happened to glance down at the studio schedule, which *happened* to be on the desk of the editorial assistant whom I *happened* to come to talk to, and there it was in black and white: Noah Adams was about to interview LUCY KAPLANSKY! I thought to myself, how many Lucy Kaplanskys can there be in the world?

But there she was at NPR in New York, her voice coming out of a speaker in Washington, talking about her life as a *singer*—she had just released her first CD—and I wanted to shout, *"Remember Ms. Goetling and her legs like mighty oaks?"*

I was glued, transfixed, hypnotized by their interview. She told Noah how she had started making a name for herself as a singer fresh out of college, but admitted she couldn't handle the success, quit, decided she wanted to go into psychology, got a Ph.D., and started to practice, only to figure out that what she really wanted to do was sing.

After all these years, it turns out, she was just as confused as me! Stumbling into adulthood unprepared for the difference between bloated expectations and actual life on earth. While I was enjoying a little neurosis, a little depression, a character disorder or two, she was . . . doing the same! Then, a few weeks after her NPR interview, she came to town for a gig. I cleared my schedule and drove to see her. I was drawn

there, pulled by a strong force—not just of nostalgia but of
sheer excitement and curiosity. Before the show started, I
went backstage, muttering to the proprietor, "You know, I've
known Lucy since she was a little pisher!" And there she
was—only now she was a big pisher. She looked exactly the
same, and I mean exactly. Hair still long, black, and wavy,
body still petite. Most striking to me were her hands. The way
she held the pen when I asked her to write down her address
and phone number was *exactly* the same way she held her
number-two pencil while taking the math test I copied off of. I
remembered it precisely. She always held her first two fingers
on the top part of the pencil, whereas I only held my
forefinger there. That was amazing to me.

She was wearing a short, sleeveless dress that immediately
made me want to ask her if she wasn't freezing in such a
skimpy thing, but I caught myself thinking, She's already got
one Jewish mother, she doesn't need two. We didn't have a lot
of time to gab, so I took my place in the audience, front row,
and waited for her to play (praying silently that she'd be really
good so I wouldn't have to come up with a huge euphemistic
lie after the show). When the lights came down and she came
out, I waited with a hard-beating heart for her to start singing.
Like what I can imagine you might feel when your child gets
up in her first school play. Not that I feel particularly maternal
toward Lucy, but I was just nervous. I wanted her to be great.
And to my great relief, she was. Her voice was like chocolate
sauce, smooth and rich and silky. And every song she sang, I
got. I didn't just get them, I *got* them. And that was just the
beginning. After the show, we were like sputtering motors,
hooting, hollering, and saying things like "Oh my *GOD!*" and
"Oh . . . MY . . . *GAWD!* Didn't you cheat off of me on that

math test once? How about the time you directly copied my geometric string design in Mr. Lubway's class, saying only, 'Imitation is the sincerest form of flattery'? Remember Miss Stribling? Whatever happened to Leo Lindo? But wait! How are you? Who are you married to? What is Spike doing these days? How about the Daskal twins—do you ever see them? . . ."

And we didn't stop talking for the rest of the night.

Now, some people you run into from your past are one-trick ponies. They are good for reminiscing with, but once you get beyond that you have nothing but your past holding you together. If you didn't know each other in that past life, you probably wouldn't be friends now. But Lucy and I, to our mutual delight, did not have this problem. The more we talked, the more we didn't have to. I would say, "How could you actually stay married for this long?" and then we'd both look at each other and simultaneously say, "Therapy!" and laugh and move on to the next area of excavation. It was like finding a long-lost sister. A twin under the skin. The toy prize inside the Cracker Jack box.

And I started to wonder: Are similar personality types, in this case neurotic Jewish females, able to recognize each other as early as second grade? Could we have possibly known that we would end up with such similarly dented psyches while we sat in a circle listening to Mrs. McCall read *Mr. Popper's Penguins*? Is the essence of the weathered thirty-five-year-old thinly veiled in the boisterous zeal of an eight-year-old? And the only conclusion I could come to was, I guess *so.*

Looking back on it now, I realize that Lucy was one of my first crushes. Girl crushes are one of the many exquisite advantages of the gender. I've had them all my life. And because they are not governed by the same strange and complicated rules of boy crushes—obsess about him, plan your strategy to make him notice you, morph into what you think he is looking for, only to find out that what he is looking for is leggy and blond—girl crushes are fantastic. Someone you think is cool, dangerous, mysterious, funny, smarter than you, a better dresser—these are perfect girl-crush candidates. They are like sweets that don't make you fat, spending that doesn't break the bank, a beautiful nap in the middle of a bad day. And it doesn't matter that a week, a month, or even twenty-two years can go by without a sighting, because the girl crush is usually for life.

Such is the case with Lucy Kaplansky.

Now, I see Lucy whenever I can. I've lived in three different cities since I reconnected with her, and each time she passes through my neck of the woods on a gig, I drag everyone I know to come hear her. She always stays with me, doing a load of wash if she needs to. If we have time, we go out for a nice meal, take a walk, or do a little shopping, and if not, I just help her carry her guitar and suitcase back to her car, point her to the highway, and watch her take off. The next time she comes to town, we have a date to go back to our elementary school and see how many new memories the building will drag out of us. I still have a crush on her and probably always will. When I went to the twentieth reunion of my elementary-school graduating class (Lucy had a gig and couldn't go), I found out I wasn't the only one. She came up as a topic of conversation among a group of girls who'd known her in kindergarten, and we all agreed that she was perfect crush material. I have had plenty of other crushes since then, but none that go so far back, and certainly none that have come full circle in such an elemental way. Girl crushes are a girl perk. It's as if the creator herself said to our kind, "Beware! your life will be hard, childbirth painful, and hormone-replacement therapy very controversial and confusing. Okay, so here's a bone, you get girl crushes . . ."

You can't really be a girl and escape them—and who would want to? Every time a great girl would breeze through my life, I was smitten. It didn't necessarily even have to be a person my age. It could have been one of my friends, one of my sisters' friends, one of my cousins' friends, one of my friends' friends, an acquaintance, or a girl on the street. Usually the most compelling part of the girl crush is that there is something about this person that is dissimilar enough to you to make her completely fascinating, yet similar enough to not be intimidating. You wonder to yourself, Could I ever be like her if I tried really, really hard? It could be something as simple as her ability to do a wheelie, her hair that hangs down below her knees, the fact that she can knock a ball out of the playground, or the way she can draw a really good horse head. Or it could be a little more exotic, like the fact that she has a pet duck named Chelveston, knows another language, or can actually keep her room clean for months at a time.

In fact, I think there is an element of a crush at the beginning of every budding friendship between girls. Some aspect or characteristic, a thing about them that captivates you and makes you want more. Years later, of course, you may realize that this person's differences from you might really drive you crazy if you had to live with them or be somehow trapped on a desert island with them, but as long as you are good friends, you can let these differences be the lure and not the unraveling of you both. This is of course why you have to be careful who you live and travel with. An exciting trip down the Colorado River could fast turn into a floating house of horror while each girl wonders what she could have possibly seen in the annoying bundle of neuroses that landed in the same raft.

Rare though it is, I have to admit there are times that tensions can arise between members of the sisterhood.

This can be a problem. It arises when girl crushes are not mutual. It's hard being on the receiving end of an unwanted girl crush. Of course, as my mother, Geraldine, says, there is a top to every pot, and for someone, this girl before you is the perfect top. Just not you, not now. This person adores you, but you would prefer vacuuming your windowsills to going out for coffee with her. Never is there a more awkward situation than this. As a member of the sisterhood it is absolutely abhorrent to be cruel or hurtful to another member, no matter how sorely you may be tempted. Someone who loves confrontation, thinks rocking the boat is the best thing since slender regulars, and has balls of steel may say something like this: "Listen, Fritzy, I have to be honest. I am really completely uninterested in maintaining a friendship with you, and in fact you are one of the many pieces of human debris that are littering my social life and cutting off my psychic circulation. I'm sorry, but I'd really love it if I never saw you again. Tootles!" It just isn't *done*.

In cases like this I usually just feign interest until said person gets married or moves away. This is a big—no, huge—problem: women who forget how to be single once they are married. There is nothing more frustrating than calling up the newly married woman and saying, "Hey, girl, how 'bout a movie on Thursday night?" and she says, "Phillip works late on Thursdays." And inside my head I'm screaming, "I don't give a rat's ass if Phillip is working late on Thursday, because

I don't want to go to a movie with *him,* you *idiot!* In fact, I have no idea why you married such a *woodhead* anyway. You are a turncoat, and if my only chance to see you has to include him, good riddance! And by the way, not only have you become someone you used to hate, but your wedding dress made you look like a baked Alaska!

A typical example of someone in this category is a person who adores you completely and unendingly. Who can respect a person like that? Naturally one must be suspicious of such enthusiasm. In all likelihood, you are just a substitute for an unfulfilled relationship of yesteryear, in which case you will be able to see the neon sign above her head that flashes NEE-DY, NEE-DY, NEE-DY. Not that someone in this group is any needier than you or me, it's just that they show it more directly, and if there is anything that we girls are trained to do from day one, it is to hide our neediness behind sparkling wit, effervescent charm, and, in short, verve.

There is no question that this can lead to many an awkward situation. But it is copable. There are ways, as we have mentioned, to get around it. Being the velvet hammer that you are, you will be the queen of tact and grace. You will come up with perfectly plausible excuses and make sure everyone is happy before severing ties. Then you can concentrate on the zillions of fascinating women worthy of crushes.

To this day, my own crushes come and go. For example, while at a benefit recently, I spied a woman on the dance floor in a skin-tight, silver-sequined cat suit. Actually, everyone spied her, since she was hard to miss. As I surveyed this exotic woman with flowing black hair and dark, dark eyes, I recognized her as someone with whom I went to junior high. She was at my Bat Mitzvah. She knew Greg Alcoke. I went running up to her and shouted out her name above the band, which was doing a respectable Sly and the Family Stone. "Cecily? Cecily Sommers!" She was stunned. I was delighted. The people I was with just rolled their eyes.

Cecily had left high school early to study dance—she was, and still is, built like a human reed. I hadn't laid eyes on her since the mid-seventies. Since then she had become a dancer, a chiropractor, a philosopher of sorts, and a gallery owner. And that was just what I got while the band was taking a break. After spending years dancing professionally, she had decided that she wanted to explore the body in a different way, including its powers to heal itself, and went to chiropractic school in Minneapolis. She stayed there, plugging into the small, hidden, but hip world of the arts there. ("Hidden" only in that New Yorkers and Californians wouldn't admit that there is anything between the coasts worth looking at, but those of us from the Midwest know better. Way better.) She became a well-respected, well-known figure in the art and chiropractic scenes in Minneapolis (her business cards show her in dance-like poses with vertebrae) and was living a happy life. And as it turned out, my instinctual radar had not failed me; she lived less than a mile away from me. We agreed to get together the following day to catch up on the past two decades.

I walked over to her house through a brisk wind and showed up on her doorstep at the appointed time. She glided to the door, taller than I will ever be in a thousand years, her hair pulled back in a bun. Now, there alone is crush material. A girl who can wear long hair past the age of twelve and get away with it is a mystery to me. She was also wearing a sweater that looked like the hide of a sheepdog, which only served to accentuate her dark features and serve as a intriguing hint of what I assumed (correctly) to be a beautiful and exotic wardrobe—another admirable quality.

As I walked into her house, opera wafted through the air, emanating from paper-thin speakers, belying a taste and sophistication anyone would admire. The house was a fantastic combination of light and air and wallpaper the likes of which I'd never seen. She spoke of Jung and the mind-body-spirit connection. She had coffee-table books of photographs so beautiful they bordered on the erotic. A Renaissance woman.

Now, in normal circumstances, being in the presence of such an enlightened aesthete would have made me want to crawl under a rock, throw away everything I ever owned, quit my job, and head for the refrigerator. But I was saved. Cecily saved me. She proved that she was not only a girl worthy of a crush for many reasons, but also that she was a girl in the *know*. Jung, shmung! She knew the words to "Love Machine"! While discussing the connection between creativity, art, depression, and madness, she broke into song, as in "I'm just a love machine and I want to work for nobody but you, *hey hey hey* . . ." and boogied around the room laughing. I knew that this was a girl of the utmost integrity. There is nothing more valuable in a friend than the dress-it-up, dress-it-down school of versatility. This was a woman whom any man or woman in their right mind would have a crush on.

We decided right then and there to join forces, join friends, join CDs, and have a joint dinner party, which turned out to be one of the best nights I had in the two years I lived in Minnesota. We served curried squash soup with apple shavings, salmon en croute, roasted beet and orange salad, and a chocolate cheesecake that could stop a heart in midbeat. People met, they shmoozed, they laughed, they ate, and the world was a beautiful place for an evening. The party was such a hit that we decided to do it on a grander scale the following year; we borrowed the warehouse studio of a photographer friend of hers, invited everyone we knew, put the Jackson 5 on the CD player, and danced like Evanston had won against New Trier in the last seconds of the game. And aside from the the fact that one of our friends was rushed to the hospital and almost died that night (allergic reaction to shrimp—but not shrimp that we served), it was a ball.

Then, a few months later, while on a four-day trip to Europe to dance at a homeopathic conference in Germany (or something like that), Cecily met a man and fell wildly in love, sold her practice, packed up her things, and moved to rural Germany with a bun in the oven. This is something that would happen only to Cecily. You gotta love that girl.

There is always room in the busiest of schedules for one more great woman, besides yourself. And once you find this woman, she is yours for life. Oh, sure, there have been girlfriends who've broken up over some major disagreement or maybe one marrying the other's ex-husband, but this is rare. A girl will go to great lengths to preserve the friendships she wants, despite the problems that may arise over the years. In this way, girl crushes last a lifetime, while boy crushes usually become sorely disillusioning. In a boy crush, the actual fall from the pedestal is an event many relationships cannot weather. In a girl crush, she never has to fall, really. You know she's not perfect, but her imperfections don't bother you. They bother *her,* and then she talks to you about it. In a boy crush, his imperfections turn out to be blinding, and you feel that if you are with this person, someone else may associate you with *his* imperfections, surely a fate worse than death. So you attack him and together you start down the road to ruin, or at least the road to lifelong bickering. In general, girlfriends don't bicker. Except when they tease each other mercilessly, like my friend Holly and me. A conversation between us may go something like this:

ME: "I want to come to New York and visit."

HER: "I have too much work, I couldn't spend much time with you. I know, maybe you could walk me to the cash machine and we could talk then."

ME: "I'm coming."

HER: "I am too busy."

ME: "I'm on my way."

HER: "Am I gonna have to get a restraining order to keep you away from me? I'm busy. I have to work twelve hours a day."

ME: "Are you going to let a little thing like work get in the way of our friendship?"

HER: "Absolutely. I can't talk now."

ME: "Who needs you to talk? I just need you to listen."

HER: "Go to hell."

ME: "Eat me."

HER: "Love you."

ME: "Love you more . . ."

This is a beautiful thing. If it were a boy and girl, they wouldn't get past date three before passing each other off as a pot without a top. But ahhhh, the girlfriend, the girl crush. There is nothing like it. And it's all *ours*.

GWGs

Hers was a character as positive as a carving knife.
—ALISTAIR COOKE

I WOULD CONSIDER MYSELF
a failure if I didn't share with you the complete array of the girl species, from those who grew up dreaming of a house in Shaumburg to those who wanted nothing more than to go on the road with Nine Inch Nails. We are a wide variety. And contained within our vast variation is a small subspecies of girl that defies nature as we know it. She is a rare puzzle. An inexplicable phenomenon. A curiosity of nature. I am, of course, talking about the Girl Without Girlfriends.

Of course, Boys Without Boyfriends aren't much better, and there are a *lot* more of these—the guys who have no confessors, confidants, or counselors until they find a nice, nurturing girl, whereupon they unburden themselves of all their deep dark secrets, neatly wrapped in a dozen long stems so that, at first, said girl is wholly flattered and touched that she alone has been trusted with such secret, deeply personal innermost thoughts, thinking to herself, He must really love me if he's telling me *this,* only to wake up six months later with a gnawing feeling that this long-suffering, ne'er-understood boy is just an asocial miscreant whose deep dark secrets are really

just festering psychoses in their Sunday best, and that his picking you as receptor of such festering psychoses is not so much
love and flattery as it is a personality disorder with a few obsessive tendencies thrown in. This means that prying him off you
is like getting rid of a parasitic tick; you may have to burn him
so that his head doesn't lodge under your skin permanently.
But that is boys, and frankly, what did you expect?

But girls . . . *girls!* Nothing can stand in the way of a girl
and her girlfriend. The strength of that bond is its own law of
physics, the eighth wonder of the world. Men worth their salt
know and respect this girl bond with just the right amount of
reverence and jealousy. But Girls *Without* Girlfriends? A
social and scientific anomaly. Let's explore.

1. A GWG is someone who gets along better with men than
   other women. This alone should send you running to yet
   again rent *Thelma and Louise*. Men love her because they
   are who she relates to best. She looks at other women
   going to the bathroom in twos and doesn't even wonder
   the teensiest bit about what is being said in there. When
   she goes to the bathroom, she actually . . . goes to the bathroom. Unheard of.
2. Girls Without Girlfriends are also girls whom men adore.
   Which proves my point about men. And because of this
   they can achieve great station in life, for they are such kin-
   dred spirits with those who compose the old-boys' network.
   Not in a Katharine-Hepburn-scrappy-tomboy-Pat-and-Mike
   kind of way, more in a Bette-Davis-emotionless-nightmare-
   Jezebel kind of way.
3. Nobody trusts a GWG worth spit. Other women can smell
   a GWG a mile away and naturally steer clear. She can feign

intimacy, like making jokes with you about your well-known sorry love life the way a real girlfriend would. But the big difference is that when you joke around about your love life with a real girlfriend, you end up feeling better about it, or if not better, at least that you're not alone and that someone empathizes. Her joking around comes complete with little conversational barbs that, when you walk away, make you feel much worse than you did before. Like, "Oh, he seems like a really good guy. *It's about time.*" Or, "I don't know how you do it. If I were single for so long, I'd *really start to worry,*" or, "Just think, a year ago I was just where you are, *single* and *lonely,* but my life has just changed one hundred and eighty degrees!" These are things that unfeeling relatives say to you, not girlfriends.

4. Girls Without Girlfriends are also girls who've never been without boyfriends. Always a red flag. They dated all through high school and college and you've often wondered how it is that they find so many dates while you spend your Saturday nights watching reruns of *The Love Boat* and eating buttered noodles. But don't worry, one day you will be a contestant on *Jeopardy* and the Daily Double will fall on this answer: "After serving on the Love Boat's crew, he ran for the U.S. House of Representatives and won." And you will pounce on your buzzer and scream, "Who is Fred Grandy!" and walk away with a new set of Samsonite luggage and a lovely new Amana range.

5. GWGs often have a thing about control. Which can work in their favor. I once knew a GWG whom we shall call Eve, as in the Three Faces of. Eve had control oozing out of her like sweat after her noon run (she was on her exercise bike at 5:45 A.M.—and this wasn't just on the Monday morning

after a particularly porky weekend, it was every day, for years on end). On the rare occasion when Eve *might* join a bunch of girls out on a mission to eat sundaes out of so many punch bowls, she would stall at the counter while everyone else ordered, pretending she was indecisive, and wait until everyone else had headed back for the table before leaning over and furtively giving the soda jerk her one word order, "Tab!" coughing up some excuse to the other women at the table, like maybe she had to have lunch with the CEO and was forced to eat a very big, heavy, late meal. She was a complicated woman, in a simple kind of way.

I knew Eve was pregnant before anyone else at work. It wasn't that she pulled me aside into the ladies' lounge and told me her news, bursting with excitement; it was that I caught her eating a whole sandwich for lunch. A whole sandwich! I immediately knew something was up. Every day for years, Eve had the same thing for lunch. Apple juice and a muffin or apple juice and a bagel. On a ravenous day, maybe apple juice and half of a sandwich, but never more. One time, when a bunch of coworkers had a party for her and brought in home-baked treats, she didn't eat so much as a grape. She didn't *want* to be a killjoy, she just couldn't help herself.

So when I saw her actually consume two whole pieces of bread with some protein in between, my mind immediately thought, Fetus! and I was right. A month or two later, when she was past the first trimester and the chances of miscarriage were minimal, she made her happy announcement and the few people with whom I had shared my prediction looked at me with astonishment. I took a bow.

Nine months later, when the baby was born, rumor had it that she was doing sit-ups the same day. That's sick—in a very Girl Without Girlfriends kind of way.

The control thing gets in the way of a GWG sharing too much of herself with you. This is because she is protective of anything said in a moment of vulnerability that could be used against her at a later date. Somehow the GWG never understood the unwritten Law of Hysteria by which you can be sobbing to your girlfriend about the misbegotten state of your affairs one minute and decide to go dancing naked in the moonlight the next. Everything is taken seriously, but you're beholden to no former feeling. Every hour you get a clean start. Those are the rules of the game. She's just never learned them.

A Girl Without Girlfriends is as easy for me to spot as a pre-1982 nose job. And like a pre-1982 nose job, there is just something distinctly artificial about her presence. Pinched and thin where it should be broad and large. Upturned where it should be straight ahead. And I think that is exactly what is so disturbing about the GWG. She has been stripped of the very characteristics that define the sex as far as I'm concerned. Warmth, camaraderie, empathy, compassion. Oh, I'm sure she still has a couple of good ovaries to her name, but I ask you, what good are they if they can't have a good cry with the ovaries in the next stall? To be a woman whom no other woman trusts, well, you might as well be a eunuch on his way to the sperm bank. It just isn't natural.

I just have to wonder how a Girl Without Girlfriends can make it through the day. If I didn't have a network of girl-friends the likes of AT&T, if their roots didn't extend far and wide like that of an ancient baobab, if I couldn't consult with them about whether to trim my hair one inch or two, I could never make it through lunch, let alone my average day. To me being without them would be like being deprived of oxygen while in the 747 nosedive that is my life. I'd be lost, I'd be despondent, I'd be a Republican. Some things you absolutely cannot go without. Water is one of them, girlfriends are another.

And like all things in life, one must be prepared for a GWG. Should you come across one, as I'm sure you will, for they are not quite as rare as one would hope, here is my advice for making it through the day. Do what any girl in her right mind would do and call a girlfriend.

BONNIE

*Shopping is better than sex. If you're not satisfied after
shopping, you can exchange it for something you really like.*
—ADRIENNE GUSOFF

A CALL TO MY GIRLFRIEND

Bonnie includes all the standards: sympathy, empathy, good gossip, and hilarity. But where she outshines the competition is in her encyclopedic knowledge of every store within a fifty-mile radius. She is, by all standards, the best, the consummate, the world's most savvy shopper. Now, I'm not talking about someone who just knows where to go for the best bargains. This woman is so far beyond your run-of-the-mill bargain hunter, Imelda Marcos would worship at her beautifully clad (for cheap!) feet. She is like the Triple Crown winner, the Nobel laureate, the decathlon champion of the world. A typical conversation:

"Bon, I need a new bra."

"What make and size?"

"Maidenform 36."

"B or C? The Bs you can get for $9.99 through Saturday at Ridgedale—taupe only—and they have four Cs left at the Outlet in white, nude, black, and pink. They're $10.89 and I wouldn't recommend the pink, it reminds me of living tissue."

I regularly get phone calls from her that sound like this: "Okay, Gwen, I'm at Marvin's clearing-house sale and I think you should come down here immediately. I'm in dressing room number four on the left. They have some fantastic Flax-like clothes for Target-like prices. You'd love them. Subtle checks, earthy colors, no seams. I'll pull a few in case you get this message in time. Or maybe I'll just buy them for you. Oh, I gotta go, someone is sniffing around my dressing room. I'M IN THERE, LADY! BACK OFF! Gotta go . . . bye!"

On her birthday, my friend Beth and I wanted to take her out for something special, like maybe a nice breakfast, time away from her kids, and a good shmooze with a lot of laughs. Naively, we didn't realize that her birthday was the same morning as Nordstrom's annual sale of the century. Naturally, this was where Bonnie wanted to go. We arranged to meet in front of the store café (Rice Krispie treats the size of bricks!) at ten o'clock. I got there first. While standing there, waiting for my bagel and cream cheese, a saleswoman came up to me and said, "Are you Beth or Gwen?" I wondered immediately if I had inadvertently been shoplifting in the four minutes I'd been there. "Bonnie asked me to come find you. She needs you down in Metrowear, room number fifteen."

"Okay," I said, feeling like a member of a shopping SWAT team, "tell her I'll be right there." When Beth arrived and I explained that Bonnie was in dire straits, we immediately hunted her down in room 15. She was surrounded by mounds of clothes and smiling saleswomen wondering what they might be able to help her with. A different size? A different color? Putting away the things she didn't want? We sat while she tried on outfit after outfit, a scene that plays out thousands of times a day all across the world.

"Too hippy," I said.

"Wrong color," Beth said.

"Nothing special," I said.

"You can do better for the price," Beth said.

"Makes you look green."

"Too much like a Nehru jacket."

"Now *that* is a keeper," we both sang.

And on the morning went, we the neophytes in the shadow of a legend. When we got separated briefly, I spotted Bonnie on her way to the dressing room, arms laden. I was about to call out to her when she boldly picked up the store intercom microphone, turned it on, and announced so the whole store could hear, "Beth and Gwen, you're needed back in the dressing room, Beth and Gwen back to the dressing roo—" She was almost done when a saleslady politely (they are never anything short of polite at Nordstrom's) pulled the mike out of her hands and led her to the New Collection for Fall.

It's like shopping is in Bonnie's blood, coursing through her veins. One time she got out the Yellow Pages, called every shoe store in town, and asked if they had a specific boot that she wanted and what the price was. When she found the lowest price, she called Nordstrom's and said, "You match prices, don't you? Good. I found this Ugg boot for eighty-three dollars at Gore's. In black. Can you match that?" They then told her that they would call Gore's to confirm and call her back. Five minutes later they called back and said they were putting a pair of black Ugg boots away for her at the special price of $83.

"Size seven and a half, right?" she asked. "Can you send them if I give you a credit card?"

"Of course!" they answered. Bonnie got the cheapest pair of Ugg boots in town in the middle of a Minnesota winter while walking around her house in fuzzy slippers and a muumuu. Brilliant.

And Bonnie's shopping acumen is as magnanimous as it is keen. She got me a pair of Ugg boots in the exact same manner, which is a good thing, since I myself can't stand buying shoes of any kind. I hate shoes. I've never understood the primal bond between women and their shoes. Women who have huge collections of shoes simply defy any kind of logic I can sink my teeth into. I've never experienced the sheer joy of finding the perfect peach pump, the thrill of taking them home, the ecstasy of wearing them out for the first time. To me, women's shoes rank up there with a full-body wax in terms of sheer torture. Sacrificing your foot to a sling-back stiletto is like voluntarily stepping into a rusty bear trap: It'll clamp onto your foot, suck the life out of it, grind your bones, smash your toes, and grate your heels like Parmesan.

I no longer shop for shoes because I wear one pair of gym shoes until my bunions have poked out the sides and the rubber is Kleenex-thin from wear and tear. If I must dress up and wear real shoes, like pumps or even Aerosoles, I take them off and store them behind the nearest potted plant as soon as I walk in the door. Perhaps I should move to Japan. But then I would miss out on shopping, the all-American endurance sport. And smart women, like you, for instance, have already figured out that the purpose of shopping is often far greater than simply purchasing things. Bonnie, the wonder shopper, knows that what you come home with in the Big Brown Bag is only part of what good shopping is all about. There is something else that happens when you shop, something curious and reassuring that I will call, for lack of a better term, shopping Zen: oxymoron to some, life maxim to others.

SHOPPING ZEN

I have to see a therapist about my retail bulimia:
shop, return; shop, return; shop, return.
                                        —BONNIE

WHEN YOU ACHIEVE THE
Zen of shopping, it can be something of a mystical experience. I don't mean that thumbing through hangers will ele-
vate you to nirvana or getting three pair of hose for the price
of two will get you any closer to a higher consciousness
(though for some it actually might—hello, Bonnie!). I mean
that there is something about the act of shopping that can
actually have inexplicable powers of restoration and healing,
despite the fact that you come home exhausted and wanting to
cut off your legs below the knee.

Now, shopping is not for everyone, and many a woman
deplores such an exhausting, materialistic, stereotypically ritu-
alistic behavior. I don't know who these women are, but I'm
sure they are out there. Even shopping haters have to admit,
however, that we're on to something here. Let me explain. I
was just talking about this with my friend Bev, who was
lamenting that a recent visit with her sister—whom she was
once close with but now felt somewhat distant from, since
their lives and personalities had taken such different paths—

was peppered with ridiculously vague, open-ended conversation that two strangers on a bus could have been having. While sitting in the kitchen, facing each other over a table, conversation was stilted with openers like, "So, how's L.A.?" A question so general as to be unanswerable except in the most general responses unbefitting sisters.

"Fine. How's Philadelphia?"

"Great. The kids are good."

"Super. What's up with Tom?"

"Nothing really, he likes his job, hates his boss, and we're thinking about buying a van."

"Nice."

"How're things with Bob?"

"Okay. Still don't know if I want to marry him or not, we'll see."

"Yeah . . . Hungry?"

"Not really."

"Oh."

"I mean unless you are. I could always eat."

"No, I'm fine."

"So, do you want to take a walk and look at some of the new stores on Maple?"

"Sure! Love to. Let me get my purse!"

And suddenly, there is excitement in the air as they both move toward a mutual activity. All at once they can talk more freely and broach subjects previously too awkward to tackle while sitting face-to-face over a little chopped liver.

Part of it, of course, is the constant distraction of looking, feeling, touching, turning tags over, trying on, comparing, debating, paying, having second thoughts, returning, and walking to the next place to do the same thing. While shopping, you may have exchanged nothing more than a few quick sentiments that are virtually meaningless, but you will both come away feeling closer because you have spent the afternoon together, doing something mutual that you have been doing since the first cavewoman decided she needed both a leopard skin and a zebra skin since some days she felt like spots and some days she felt like stripes.

This inexplicable bonding thing is there, in some way, right between the NO SHIRT, NO SHOES, NO SERVICE sign and the basket of peds for those trying on black suede pumps. It is unspoken, and that is the beauty of it. The mere act of going shopping together proves that you still have a connection to this person, no matter how tenuous that connection is in other circumstances. This rule does not apply if you stop for lunch, dessert, or coffee, since you are back at the table experiencing one-on-one ambivalence and the aforementioned face-to-face awkwardness. My suggestion is that you always shop on a full stomach. That way, of course, you not only avoid the desire to stop for snacks and libations, but you also shop at your fattest and can then really pat yourself on the back when you get the pants home a few hours later and they already feel a little looser.

My friend Leslie equates it to riding in a car with someone and having a conversation that you would not be able to have outside of the car because in the car you are in the same space but cannot really look at each other, which provides a buffer zone in which difficult topics can be broached. She remembers the time driving in the car with her mother when she finally came out with something she'd been terrified to tell her at any other time. "I'm taking birth control pills, Mom," she said, waiting for the ax to fall. Her mother was clearly deeply affected by her confession.

"Thank *God*," she replied, and the two went on their merry way (her mom was always so cool).

The miraculous act of shopping can open new gateways of intimacy even for the best of friends. And, depending on where you shop, it can be a lot cheaper than therapy. If you are a Loehmann's shopper, this would be the shopping equivalent of group therapy. This group dressing room is not for the faint-hearted (which is why the men sit out on the couch near the door with a glazed look in their eyes as though the taxidermist had already gotten to them). There are more folds in the Loehmann's dressing room than in an origami lotus garden. And if you are a girl who can appreciate the flavor of the experience without running out in horror at seeing your future in control tops, this is just the place for you. Front-row views of uncorralled stomachs sprawling into the great beyond, breasts the size of highway cones. And there is something truly beautiful about it. It is what we are before we do any exterior decorating. It is who we are, like it or lump it. Literally. The sheer variety of directions a body can go is so remarkable. There before you stand examples of every size and shape of the female form, dimpled, wrinkled, and varicose. You gotta love it. And you do. Otherwise you would throw yourself in front of the nearest train. The Loehmann's dressing room facilitates discussion among strangers like no other. You can come away with not just a second and third opinion but a blind date with the woman in the red pantsuit's grandson (the medical student!) and a recommendation for a lunch spot where they serve an abundance of free bialys.

Like therapy, shopping can be a cleansing experience. I can still remember when I had a knock-down, drag-out fight with my mother years ago. Afterward, we went shopping. For what, I don't remember. A tangible pick-me-up, I think (fortunately, we have similar taste and shopping styles, although back then I heard a lot of "Jeez, Gwen, couldn't you pick something a little more *exciting*?"). I remember at the time thinking that it was a really strange activity to take up just after a brutal battle, but it did the trick. Smoothed over the wounds and paved the way for me to go back home with a feeling that all was not lost. And we are not alone. Of the millions of mothers and daughters and sisters who darken the doors of malls and boutiques every day, you can bet that a good number of them aren't talking about much more than the weather or how Uncle Morry was incontinent in his final days, but nevertheless coming away feeling quite cozy and satisfied with one another.

Of course, boys will never be able to have quite the connection that women feel while shopping, if for no other reason than that they usually go into the dressing rooms one at a time. This may explain why they dress the way they do. What's the point of even entering a store if you are forced to try things on alone? I have been known to pull total strangers from browsing the sales racks for a second opinion. There is nothing quite as discouraging as having to trust yourself in trying to determine if the little black dress whispers "Come hither" or shouts "One too many sheet cakes."

Likewise, men do not understand the finer, more restorative aspects of shopping. They just look at the bills and roll their eyes. And if you say to them, "But honey, it did wonders for our relationship," they will just look at you as though you are one M&M short of a full pack. Maybe shopping is the female equivalent to watching a football game, where all attention is focused on an impersonal object so nothing of an intimate nature need be exposed. Personally, I'd rather watch Bonnie run down eighty yards' worth of Nordstrom's aisles than watch Steve Young on the football field. What does he come away with? A ball and six points. In eighty yards, Bonnie could provide you with a whole new fall look for the price of your ticket in the end zone. Besides, is Steve Young going to fill you in on his newest theory of what his last relationship taught him about the nature of sex and intimacy as it relates to his long repressed hostility toward his mother (with whom he is going shopping next week)? Not hardly.

So the next time anyone (he) gives you a hard time about a shopping trip, you just stand up and shout, "Hey, I'm paving over emotional potholes here, bub, cut me some *slack!*" This could very well inspire the newspaper reaction, where he turns away from you and buries his head in the newspaper, pretending that he is a well-read intellectual up to date on the most current of current events, when in fact he is merely avoiding the subject, since emotional potholes aren't something he really feels like discussing right now. But that's okay. When he hoists it in front of his face and snaps it crisply to emphasize his disdain, just remember to position yourself strategically to get a good view of the back page, so you can make a mental note of all the sales.

THE OVA OFFICE

Now they're advertising breathable pantyliners. You know
some man invented that product. No woman would be
inventing a pantyliner and putting little holes in there.
She'd be putting little tongues in there.

—DIANE FORD

DRESSING ROOMS, FAN-
tastic though they are, have their limitations. For they are only
runners-up, second-placers, the Miss Congenialities of facilities.
If you are interested in the fine art of girl talk (and what girl
worth her salt isn't?), then for the ultimate, the very Mecca of
locales that beckon to women of all makes and models, we turn
to the fabulous, the magnificent, the exalted Ladies' Lounge, for
which nothing short of hosannas can express due praise.

The ladies' lounge is where it all goes down. Maybe it's the
acoustics. Maybe it's just that while you strip your body bare,
you strip your soul bare as well. If you go to the bathroom in
twos, the very greatest of female traditions (and of course usually both women don't *need* to go, only one needs to go and the
other is just along for the ride, since you never know what kind
of great stuff is going to be unearthed in the bathroom) then
you are a walking illustration of the notion that I think of as
the cement, the very Krazy Glue of girlfriendship: shared

intimacy. Shared intimacy and shared privacy, oxymorons only a woman could love. Some people—Lord knows who—think that privacy should actually be private. Privacy, shmivacy, I say. What's the point? If you're going to be in a mirrored space, viewing the transformation of your body from something peachy to something hairy, lumpy, and pocked, wouldn't you rather do it among friends? Of course you would.

This tradition begins early on. From the time your mommy sits you on the potty for the first time, the bathroom is a place to be with others. A classroom for the young female mind and body. This is where you learn at the bare feet of your sisters, who sit on the edge of the tub while you are at the sink. They can show you everything from brushing the tangles out of your hair after the bath to the best way to pop a zit without leaving a scar. You can watch to see how they shave their legs, apply their eye shadow, examine their teeth, talk on the phone (now, with portables, it's so much easier), preen, prance, and pose. When I was teetering toward puberty, my older sister and my older cousin would dance around the bathroom comparing breast size and shape ("Me big tit, you little tit!") while teasing me about the darkening peach fuzz in my crotch. Nothing was off limits. When needed, we changed tampons as casually as checking the mirror for dandruff. One time, when my curiosity could be contained no longer (being the late bloomer that I was), a good-natured girlfriend of mine agreed to show me what a used tampon looked like after she removed it (later, her boyfriend had the same curiosity, so I didn't feel as perverse). She did so with these words of advice: "Always pee *before* you change your tampon, or you could end up peeing on your hand." A wise woman, she.

This is the way bathrooms are. Halls of higher learning, if you will. When I was a girl, we wouldn't dream of interrupting a delicious conversation just to go to the bathroom. So, instead, we just all went together, and years later, nothing much has changed. Except maybe the nature of the conversation. It began with boys, boys, boys, and continued on with boys, sex, fat. Now it continues with boys, sex, fat, with an occasional "How's that irritable bowel?" thrown in. Fortunately, this is lifelong.

If it is a bathroom in someone's home, then the conversations can be intensely intimate. As in talking about the people in the living room. It is a safe haven because the people they are talking about will never come in—it is, after all, a bathroom. And the acoustics being what they are, you can speak in a barely audible whisper and still be heard. Home bathrooms are excellent for sharing secrets. How many times have you been at a party and grabbed (or been grabbed by) a girlfriend, yanked her upstairs to the bathroom, sat her down, and said, "You are not going to *believe* what Shlomo just said to Justine! He told her he was in love with her! But what about Shirley? She'll be crushed. Should we tell her? You tell her—no, I'll tell her. What do you think she'll do if we tell her? We have to tell her. Wouldn't you want to know? I'd want to know . . ."

This is called The Review, a most popular bathroom pastime. Bathrooms are the perfect spot to check in with each other throughout the evening to review any given situation, be it family gathering, dinner party, chess club, or whatever. This is done quite a bit in restaurants, as in the classic scene of two women going to powder their noses—translation: talk about the men they are with. In a restaurant, you can stay gone for only so long before they send a search party. Generally speaking, home bathrooms are the most intense; however, sometimes the intimate conversation just expands to fit a larger setting and include a greater number of women. In a bathroom at work, for instance (four stalls, four sinks, and a connected room that has a couch and a lot of mirrors. The couch-in-the-bathroom thing used to be there, I believe, to provide respite for women feeling faint from their monthly difficulty. Now that women's monthly difficulties seem to be less difficult, the couches are leather invitations to set a spell and have a good chaw with your fellow worker) two women were once talking about the upcoming wedding of one of them and all of the rigmarole that was going into it, particularly the dress that she'd bought. Naturally, everyone there chimed in with what she wore at her wedding, how ridiculous she felt, and what kind of scandals one ballsy woman caused when she picked a backless number and could hear people gasp as she passed them going down the aisle (she particularly remembered the sound of her mother-in-law gasping). The chiming in was done from everywhere: the sink, the stalls, the couch, the floor. This, by the way, is something men are flabbergasted by, that women talk to each other while in the stalls. Of course they do. Why waste a minute of precious talking time? Why don't men talk in the stalls? That's what I think is much more worthy of inquiry and note.

Big deal, you might think, who cares about hearing stupid wedding-dress stories? And I couldn't agree more. But then this indicates that you've missed the entire point. Because what you are forgetting about is that when you are in the women's room and women are present, the stories only *start* at the wedding dress. They will morph into honeymoon stories, marital advice, secrets about their husbands they are willing to divulge only because they are in the bathroom and not the hallway, clandestine affairs they've had, divorces, children, child rearing, aging parents, the quark as a particle and what it can tell us, the election of Jesse "the Body" Ventura, and so on. Everything you can think of has been discussed in the ladies' lounge.

And done. Total makeovers from ratty jeans to glamour queen, including hot rollers, makeup, sponge bath, and nails. I have seen people cry their eyes out, sleep, cut their hair, brush their teeth, puke, decorate cakes, pump milk from their breasts, work, compare undergarments, show off new clothing, talk on the phone, argue with their boyfriends who were waiting outside, reprimand their children where they think they won't be seen, get into fights, smoke, wash out birth control devices, stand sideways at the mirror to see if their stomach is any flatter now that they've just eliminated eight ounces of urine, collate their thesis, eat something before dinner so that they don't consume as much food on a date (and thereby not show yourself to be the pig that you are), take money out of ungodly places you would never think that money could fit into comfortably, hug and comfort one another, give fashion advice, exchange the names of good hairstylists, dole out feminine-hygiene products to women without quarters, read, and even go into labor. The bathroom has seen it all.

The ladies' lounge is like the international clubhouse for girlfriends. You can be in any city, any state, any country, and receive the same warm shoulder to cry on when your date has just told you you have thick ankles. An interchange that begins with "Could you hand me a paper towel?" could easily proceed to "Well, after my divorce, I went into a profound depression and put on forty pounds, which my therapist attributes to low self-esteem." Everything is fair game, nothing is sacred. A simple glance in the mirror that results in the muttering under one's breath of an innocent "I would love to lose ten pounds before the summer" can unleash a flurry of body berating. Like a Greek chorus, the women in the room will rise up and join in.

"Oh, please, I should be so fat," one will say. "I mean, if my hips were any wider I could swim in the Atlantic and Pacific and the same time!"

"*You!* My eyelids are beginning to dimple!"

"Excuse me," another one will chime in. "Look at these upper arms, they're halfway to the floor." And on and on and on.

It's an ageless, timeless, and thoroughly dependable tradition. Test it out. Next time you're in a public rest room, throw out the words "stretch marks" and see what happens.

The universal language of women, that instant kinship that strikes among four X chromosomes, is unparalleled. Not that men don't have some advantages in life. They can pee their names in the snow and they don't have to wait in long lines to get into the john. But that's fine with me, because when it comes to getting into the women's room, it's well worth the wait.

VANITY HAIR

I refuse to think of them as chin hairs.
I think of them as stray eyebrows.
—JANETTE BARBER

WHEN A GIRL IS IN THE
ladies' room, be it at home, at work, or at the Metropolitan
Museum of Art, it is absolutely assured that she will regularly
check herself in the mirror for one thing: chin hair. There's
nothing a girl likes worse than finding a chin hair. Now, I'm
not talking about that baby-fine peach fuzz that carpets your
body like velvety moss. I'm talking about those thick, black,
wirelike hairs. Spiky hairs that poke through your skin like a
thorny cactus in smooth desert sand.

This is the legacy I inherit from my father: an overabun-
dance of unwanted body hair. It's his Eastern European heritage. There, it's not so unwanted. Here, it's just considered
"indelicate" to walk around looking like a human Chia Pet. Of
course, if you fall victim to societal dictum, you can spend a
lot of time and money shaving here, bleaching there, tweezing
this and waxing that. Hair is relentless, brutal in the way it
sprouts up where it's not wanted. Shave your legs and sure,
they may look good for a couple of hours. Then comes the five
o'clock shadow, then the sandpaper, then the old-growth forest.

I don't understand these women with no body hair. Who are they? Blondes, certainly. Jews? Never. Run a potato up my legs and it slices, dices, makes julienne fries.

Men, of course, can be just as hairy as they want to be. Miniature hair fountains spring from their ears and cascade from their noses. Their eyebrows could form a hair equator around their heads and no one would say a word. They've never heard of bikini burn, they don't know Jolene from Eileen. I ask you: Just how many men even know the meaning of the word "depilatory"?

They have no clue. In bathrooms all over the country, roommates, sisters, mothers, girlfriends, and wives are locking the door, hunting for hair, going in for the kill, and emerging smooth as a bowling ball. It is a true benchmark of intimacy to depilate in front of another person.

I myself used to be happy picking, plucking, and pulling my chin hairs out one by one in the privacy of my own home until I made the mistake of merely greeting my sister, the *doctor,* one day in a brightly lit room. With her, a mere perfunctory salutation is an open invitation for a baboonlike grooming. There is not a zit, a dandruff flake, a wart that escapes her. On this occasion she took one look at me, dragged me into a private corner, stared at my chin, and said two words: *"Don't pluck!"*

What is she, crazy? I love plucking. There's nothing more gratifying than pulling a big black hair out of your chin by the roots, like an evil weed.

"It just grows back WORSE!"

This is one of the all-time greatest urban myths, which, to my knowledge, has never been proven. But that doesn't stop every older sister, baby-sitter, and *Seventeen* magazine columnist from perpetuating it. I remember a camp counselor of mine begging me never to shave my legs, for fear of a lifetime of misery. Coming from my sister the doctor, it had a little more scientific weight behind it, though I strongly suspected that in all her fellowships in opthalmology and cornea transplants, permanent hair removal hadn't come up much as a topic for scientific study, except maybe in a gathering of female residents in the bathroom in the middle of the night. Nevertheless, I heeded her warning. I envisioned myself with a goatee.

"Do what I do," she said. "Go see Rae."

Rae? Who's Rae? Turns out, Rae was an electrolysist. In Skokie. Now, Skokie is not a place you want to go for many things unless you have a hankering for extra lean corned beef on rye. But I went. In Rae's house not a tchotchke was out of place. She had things like glass and ceramic figurines that doubled as candy dishes and soap holders. She had tea cozies on the teapots, plastic wrap on the furniture, and a naggingly pervasive smell of soap and old-people's home wafting through the air. Her office was in the basement, so her door was always open and clients came and left as they needed to. I ventured down to the basement, which can be properly described only as a rumpus room complete with knotty pine paneling, an old Ping-Pong table, and pictures of her children, now grown, all over the walls. I waited my turn on her sofa while I wondered just what was going on behind that pseudo-Japanese screen that separated the waiting area from her working area. Finally, it was my turn. She was wearing a white nurse's uniform, which gave me an odd feeling of comfort, until she had me lie down on the examining table and yanked back my head.

"You know," she said, "you're worse than your sister."

That's the way things go in my family. I am the victim of a snowballing set of traits that gather strength as they get passed down. As the youngest of four, I got the lion's share of imperfections, not the least of which is an abundance of unwanted body hair.

Rae's nimble fingers scanned the hair on my chin as though it were braille and she were a speed reader. Like a pointillist with an electric pen, she zapped each and every hairy pore. For twelve minutes a week, I became a human pincushion. I would lie there, staring at the ceiling, counting the tiny holes in her corkboard-made-to-look-like-marble drop-ceiling tile, wondering which had more holes at the moment, the ceiling or my chin. I would wait for the kitchen timer to go off, signaling the end of my session. Every week I paid her the same amount and every week she said the same thing: "Don't *pluck!*"

Eventually, the hair went away. But then, eventually, the hair grew back. It always does. Good-bye Yul Brynner, hello Cousin It. Now, I know that in the big scheme of things, it's neither hair nor there, but I can't help but wonder, why me? I decided to go right to the source: my father. I called him up and came right to the point.

"Dad, I have a question for you. Why are we so hairy?"

"What?"

"Why are we so *hairy?*"

"*We* aren't, *you* are maybe."

Subtlety has never been my father's strong suit.

"You have black hair," he continued. "That doesn't help. But I'm not so hairy, am I?"

"No," I admitted.

"A little hair on my chest maybe," he added. "You are just an aberration, that's all, heh heh heh . . ."

An aberration. Was that the best he could do? I wanted answers. There were none to be found. I haven't been back to electrolysis since. I've thought about it, but the idea of someone sticking a hot electrode into my pores is somehow less appealing than it once was. Which leaves me doing a daily check of newly sprouted wanton hairs. It all boils down to this: If I were stranded on a desert island and I could bring only three things, sure, the first two would be food and water, the sustenance of life, but food, shmood, no girl in her right mind would even step onto that desert isle without that which is absolutely essential to her survival, key to her very existence, a life-and-death acquisition of the utmost import: a silver, sure-grip, slant-point, lightweight, easily-concealed-in-a-pocket-or-purse, seek-and-destroy tweezers. And to those jet-black, needlelike hairs just waiting to erupt from an otherwise smooth and beautiful chin, I have only two cautionary words: pluck you.

SACRED LOVE WAND
OR SNAKE IN THE GRASS?

I once dated a guy who was so dumb he couldn't count to twenty-one unless he was naked.

—Joan Rivers

OF ALL THE THINGS THAT make up a girl's life, I think it would be fair to categorize most of them into two groups: things done and things yet to do. And that is exactly how the years pass—waiting for certain milestones (like blue eye shadow) to come by so you can leap over them with joy and delight in your own maturity. Things like shopping—that is a given, since you've been doing it since you could walk. Slow-dancing with Greg Alcoke—that was a biggie, since it was preceded by such great anticipation. And so things go until you wake up one day and realize that the only thing left for you to experience is walking toward a bright light.

Some of these experiences are best left a mystery, so that each and every girl has to feel it out and make it her own. But others . . . well, I would be remiss if I left any girls to fend for themselves without a few words of precaution. Into this category falls the most curious of things, the penis. No discussion of the things close to a girl's heart would be complete without a few words about it. Not that a penis is necessarily close to a woman's heart—an odd configuration at best. It's just that a girl can't get too old without thinking that a man's love thang and his relationship to it are just so damned odd. Is there anything stranger? Don't think so. And since so much of a girl's time is spent wondering at, guessing about, investigating, and finally experiencing said penis in all its many forms and manifestations, it ends up being close to a woman's heart by default, if nothing else.

The first time I touched a man's penis, I was slightly alarmed. Not by what it felt like, but by the fact that I was touching *it*. This was a real milestone. And when a milestone is in process, it's just impossible to be "in the moment." I was too preoccupied that this was actually happening to *me* to do anything but become the third-party observer, dissociating from myself but taking careful mental notes. They read, "Disgusting!"

At times like this I'm like a hound dog, hearing things that only dogs can hear, smelling things only dogs can smell, seeing things . . . well, you get the picture. And it doesn't have to be a sexual milestone by any means. The first time I got beat up I felt the same way. It happened one day early in my career at a new school, in a new town that I'd just moved to. We were playing some kind of bombardment-like game and Janet Smith, an eighth-grader who towered over me and snapped her gum like a frenzied metronome, grabbed the ball, yanking my long hair along with it. And while I am sure this was unintentional, I nevertheless decided (uncharacteristically) to chart my territory, like a dog pissing in a big circle. That was when I made the fatal error. I turned to her and said, "Watch it!" like a new girl who could afford eighth-grade enemies eight inches taller and twenty pounds heavier. And that, apparently, was like putting a bull's-eye on my back. In the locker room after gym, Jackie threatened that she was going to kick my ass, and by God, she was good to her word. While walking up the stairs back to class, she started punching me in the back. I'm sure they weren't more than strong shoves, but I remember them as cartilage-crunching blows. And at the time Jackie was using my back as a punching bag I didn't think about how much it hurt or how humiliated I would be when my mother called the school and I had to meet with Jackie while Mr. Auburn (the school counselor who yearned for camaraderie with the students, but whose 1972 goatee belied his complete and total dorkiness) made us "recon-cile," making me a walking target for the rest of the year. No, I thought only, This girl is beating me up, I can't believe it!

But penis touching was a big one. Not a big one per se, but you catch my drift. A milestone big enough that it had to be shared and shared alike. And for those of us who reached cer-tain milestones first (even though I felt "behind" as a junior in high school) we had an unspoken obligation to go back and tell those still waiting what to expect. In this case I distinctly remem-ber a friend calling me up to ask about my date while my whole family was milling about so I could talk to her only sporadically.

"Yeah, Mom, the table is set and the water is boiling, I *touched* it, and yes, the pasta is in."

"You *touched* it?!" she gasped. "Oh my God! Tell me every-thing. Everything! What did it *feel* like?" A natural question. I thought about it for a moment. Not too easy to describe. This was the best I could come up with:

"It felt like a hot dog," I whispered. "A frozen one."

Upon entering this strange and vast world of the penis, a girl should be as prepared as she can be, but ultimately, it could be just another milestone, less fantastic than some peo-ple would have you believe. Because to men it may feel like their whole body is a human firework, but from the outside, it still just feels like a hot dog. And for God's sake, don't fall for the bun argument whatever you do.

My first close-up experience with a penis (after that first hot-dog handshake), the first one I saw walking around unabashedly in broad daylight belonged to a man I met my freshman year of college. His name was John. He was boisterous and gregarious and had a big smile and an easy laugh. A nice Jewish boy. With shoulders yet. Though he lived down the hall, we didn't get to know each other until well into the first semester, when of course every single person on campus is a potential notch on your proverbial bedpost. And then one day, out of the blue, he stopped hanging around his friends (who didn't get—or didn't want—housing in the dorms and ended up in towerlike apartments that housed, like, 90 percent of the Jewish freshmen), and started hanging out with us. All of a sudden there was this handsome, charismatic guy living down the hall, kidding around, gesturing dramatically, and ribbing the hell out of me. And there is nothing I like better than to be made fun of, it's true. (It runs in the family, as it turns out. Imitate my father, John, and one of his many idiosyncratic habits, and tears roll down his cheeks. He stops breathing completely, making repetitive staccato glottal sounds like a human metronome, eh-eh-eh—eh-eh-eh. I'm the same way.) If you are funny enough and can really throw a few zingers my way, I am putty in your hands. Since we were both from the same area, he offered to take me out for my birthday after we went home for winter break and before he left with his family for (where else?) Florida. John was a playboy, the kind who can get away with too much because of his good looks and jaunty demeanor. Like the time months later I told him he was acting like an asshole and he said, "You're right." And I said, "Well, if you are aware that you are acting like an asshole, then don't act like one!" This proved to be too large a request, but let's not spoil the story of the first date with the details of the self-centered boorishness that reared its ugly head down the road.

Naturally, my biggest concern about the evening was what to wear. And so I flung my clothes around the room all afternoon, trying them on in different combinations. Now, even for a seventeen- (almost eighteen-) year-old, running around in nylons and a bra is, to say the least, unflattering. To say nothing of degrading, depressing, and cold. And, for some long-forgotten reason, I had no girlfriend there to tell me that the blue dress was too Florence Henderson and my sister's Qiana jumper was too Princess Leah. This is a bad state of affairs when one is going on a big date with a big guy. I was left to decide for myself, a terrifying notion, and was still throwing things on when the doorbell rang. In my hurry to get dressed before opening the door (since I thought that opening the door in my underclothes might scare him away for good), I threw on some socks, a skirt (my sister's), a blouse (my sister's), and boots (it was still the seventies, you know) and was forced to leave on the offensive panty hose (this was way before the era of tights or leggings, when panty hose could be so tight as to cause life-threatening blood clots).

John came to the door in a beautiful charcoal-gray camel-hair suit, crisp white shirt, dark hair, and sparkling green eyes. It was impressive. And he was in his element. He loved just this kind of setup—taking a girl out to somewhere she'd never been, in this case a fancy-shmancy place called Eugene's, leading all the way. May I take a moment here to add that this is not at all a bad way to go? Dinner was beautiful, the company was entertaining, the wine was expensive, and the waiter brought me a piece of cheesecake with a candle in it for my birthday (is there a better way to get into a girl's pants?). We then started back toward home, stopping for gas along the way.

Thinking ahead while he pumped the gas, I knew that if I was lucky, the night was not going to end at the front door. I also knew that I would rather take a bath with a downed telephone wire than be wearing panty hose when a man touched my waist. This is a girl's worst nightmare, and I don't see how Republicans, who seem always to be wearing panty hose, even in their sleep, can carry it off. For no matter how skinny you might be, nylons in 1978 pinched your waist so tightly that they forced all the fat in your body to be squeezed up from your toes, spilling over the waistband cinch like a mushroom cloud of flesh, rendering you a human popover. So, while I was watching my date pump gas on that cold December night, I decided to take off my boots, take off my socks, take off my nylons, and put my socks and boots back on, all before he got back to the car. It was a challenge, but this was not a problem. I can do anything in a car: change my clothes while eating lunch on the interstate, no problem. Balance my checkbook while cleaning out the backseat in rush hour? Please.

When we got to my house, we built a fire and curled up in front of it. We laughed and smooched and laughed some more. It got late and my date had an early plane, so we called it an evening, and after suffering a good dose of beard burn, I was left with an unusually strong yen to get back to school.

It was late when he left, and I went up for but a few hours of sleep before I was awakened by a phone call from him. John called to tell me that his mother had just popped her head into his room with my nylons in her hand, saying, "John, dear, would you know anything about these?"

Thus began a romance that would last just short of a year. And in the spring, I decided that the ultimate mystery of life for a girl of eighteen had to be unraveled. I decided that my virginity was made to be lost. I was later told that my family had been discussing the matter without me. Apparently my brother asked my father if he thought I was sleeping with John, who by this time had gotten to know the family pretty well. My father, in his inimitable way, replied, "I certainly hope so," and went back to his architectural drawing board.

I dutifully went to my gynecologist for a diaphragm fitting, being possibly the most paranoid person in the world in regard to birth control. Since my mother's gynecologist was far away—she stuck with him out of loyalty—I went to a gynecologist who'd come recommended by my mother's younger, hip friend (this recommendation was the sole blot on her otherwise untainted image for me). He was an older, straitlaced man who could always be relied on for two things: telling you how much weight you'd gained since your last visit and waiting until your legs were widespread in the stirrups before making small talk like "So, what are you studying in school this year?" I have never seen a male gynecologist since.

Back on campus, I had seen signs for a "Caribbean Getaway" dance and, convinced that we would win the one trip to the Caribbean and that that would certainly be worth suffering through a few hours of drunken frat boys and bouffy sorority girls, I, in an act that belied my naïveté, bought tickets and went with my green-eyed intended. The night was a total bust. Boring people, bad music, and guess what? We didn't win. But we had a room at the student union, which also served as a hotel to parents, visitors, and virgins waiting to be deflowered. We retired for the night and prepared for the big event. Now, as any girl knows, the art of putting in a diaphragm must be perfected over time and cannot be mastered without a few mishaps involving small beige saucers catapulting out of your hand and making a long and slippery arc across the length of the bathroom. And you may as well be giving your engine a lube job for all the mess you end up making. If there's anything that can kill romance, it's diaphragm insertion. But, as this was a much anticipated event for both parties involved, it went ahead as scheduled.

I have two overriding memories of the evening: pain and guilt. The pain was what instantly made me wonder what the hell everyone was so obsessed about. Was *this* it? Because basically, it sucked. Was this one of those beer/wine/acquired taste kinds of things? I took mental notes. They read, "Don't ever do this again."

Then there was the guilt. What would my mother do if she found out? I was sure she would keel over and die, her premature death forever on my head, specifically my libido. Call it sick, call it twisted, call it Jewish, whatever, that is what I remember, other than him running around naked in the morning with his penis bouncing around openly and me staring in amazement at his lack of embarrassment. I wanted to remind him, "You know, your penis is just hanging there out in the open for everyone, like me, to see." But you could tell he really didn't care a whole lot. His lack of inhibitions— especially compared to my stockpile—was refreshing. I liked him. He liked me. Everything went along swimmingly.

Until he broke up with me and took up with a very skinny girl who badly dislocated her jaw one day when she was jogging around a running track while chewing sugar-free gum. Served him right for breaking up with a jewel such as myself.

There was long dry spell after that, but a little later things picked up. Okay, a lot later—after I'd dropped out, worked for two years, and transferred schools. Then penises just became a lot more common. I don't mean to say that some men started growing two or three, just that after a while, a girl just sort of gets used to them, strange beasts though they are. Then conversations no longer include exclamations like "I touched it!" because of course, that becomes presumed. Weathered women instead have conversations that sound like this:

"How'd things go last night with Mark?"

"Fine. He named his penis."

"Oh no, not another one."

"You'd think it was a Cabbage Patch Kid or something."

"What was it this time?"

"You wouldn't believe it if I told you."

"Try me."

"Sir, Your Highness."

And peals of laughter ring out for blocks and blocks.

I can tell you this much. I would never want to be a guy. Too weird. Actually, I would, for a few days, to see what all the hoopla is about, but after that, give me internal plumbing any day. Much more, shall we say, subtle. I mean, it's a good thing penises are out there. Just as long as they stay well behaved. Maybe a leash is what's called for, or periodic signs telling their owners to clean up after their nuisances or suffer a fine.

But despite their wily nature, penises are things the world cannot do without. We can do without them for plenty of years in a row and be perfectly happy. But every once in a while, a girl can have a hankering. A yearning. And in the smorgasbord of life, sometimes a hot dog is just what a girl is in the mood for.

PART 2
LOVE
& HISSES

If brevity is the soul of wit, your penis must be a riot.

—Donna Gephart

WHEN IT COMES TO MEN, WHAT CAN YOU SAY?

Volumes. However, in my opinion, life with men is best summed up by my wise sister who said, succinctly, "He'll never be your girlfriend, so don't get your hopes up."

If a girl as smart as yourself really wants to dig into the matter and truly get to know the nature of men and therefore boys, let me save you a lot of time and effort that you would otherwise spend trying to evaluate their intellectual motivations, their emotional states, and the reasons behind their inexplicable behavior. The thing to do is to take the anthropological view, try to concentrate on just how it is that they develop into the people they are: that is to say, thinly veiled sperm distributors. It will open up a wealth of answers. An ocean of understanding. And all you have to do is look down.

The penis, as we know, is a strange and unpredictable animal. But still, it wasn't until I grew way up and watched as my nephews and friends' sons started running around naked at the ages of two, three, four, and five that I came to fully understand men's preoccupation with their groins. A boy (a younger one especially) runs around holding on to his penis, waving it, bending it, pretending it's a gun or a hose or a sword, with unabashed pride. It's like he has his own built-in toy box that goes with him everywhere. A handle he can hold on to whenever he wants. For comfort, for pleasure, for play (not foreplay). Even the boys who don't outwardly revel in these objects of curiosity have to give them some guidance every day just to pee. Touching his penis is *required* of a boy. It is a part of his everyday repertoire. No wonder boys are obsessed. And then, at some point, when they make the connection between touching and pleasure, well, magnanimous people that they are, they want everyone to share in their good fortune. How generous! Really. And watching those young, naked, unabashed penis grabbers in their youth makes the men they turn into seem almost logical. It all comes together. Built-in toy turns joystick turns alter ego. A natural progression.

I was never more reminded of this than when I went to a gay bar in Washington, D.C., with a friend of my then boyfriend, now husband, Paul. Burt was visiting us in D.C. and was sick and tired of the same old bars that he'd been to a thousand times, and I had heard much said about this one particular place. I was told that it was a club where men danced totally nude on the bar, and then some. That was all I needed to hear. For Burt and me, this was like dangling candy in front of a three-year-old. We were on our way. Paul, to his credit, came along to be a good sport (he knew he would be labeled as a boring penis-phobe if he stayed home) and put the best face on the experience he could. Our other houseguest at the time, a man undergoing confirmation hearings for a very high government office, thought it better to stay home.

The description I had been given turned out to be dead on. Burt, a gay man living in San Francisco yet, recoiled with shock upon walking in, let out a high-pitched "Oh my *Gawd!*" and turned to go. I would have none of this, and pulled him back in with this advice: "Just think of it as a smorgasbord." We fought our way through the crowd. The floor was crowded with patrons, and on the bar were nude men of all sizes, shapes, and colors. Nude, that is, save for their socks. Health regulations, I guess. They swayed and danced to the music, fondling themselves gently to keep themselves in a semierect or erect state all night. Ah, youth.

This was the first time I noticed that the socks served multiple purposes. Not only did they protect the bar from whatever moldy spores find their way onto the human foot, they also acted as purses of sorts. Think about it. If you had to fondle yourself all night, you'd need some provisions too. After a rousing fondle, sometimes to the beat of the music (no pun intended), a little lubrication was in order to avoid the chafing that seemed inevitable. So all the dancers kept a small vial of balm, looking a lot like lip gloss, in their socks. And occasionally they would bend down, get it, and nonchalantly apply it directly to their love wands.

They were proud wranglers. Happy to be seen, happy to be erect, happy to be getting paid. They were smiling and they

were relaxed. Like so many boys on broomstick horses, they
rode their steeds mightily, as if to say to the world, "Isn't my
pony resplendent?" The sheer glory of it all was really quite
awesome. A penis-fest among penis appreciators. There was
the boyish-looking blond sucking on the hood string of a
windbreaker he was wearing to add to his coyish, boyish
appeal, the muscle man (incidentally, the least well endowed),
the S&M guy in the leather and chains in the corner, and the
John Dillinger look-alike. It was hard to take your eyes off this
last guy. He was truly astonishing. Fourteen inches long if he
was an inch. It was like a long sausage at the deli counter,
enough to feed twenty. It was really mesmerizing. Like the
three-hundred-pound pumpkins at Halloween you pass and
think to yourself, How is that possible? Even Burt was completely taken aback by this. "Ouch" was all he could say.

And then I noticed that the chorale of wranglers had
turned into a sort of penile petting zoo. Every once in a while,
a patron at the bar would position himself right underneath
the dancer and slip a dollar or a fiver into the dancer's sock
(they do come in handy, don't they?) in the great tradition of
the G-string tipper. But this was not just a few bucks given in
appreciation of this dancer's sense of rhythm; no, this was a
barter. For the one, five, or ten dollars that they would fold
lengthwise and slip into the sock would buy the patron a
chance at a good fondle. The dancer would crouch down and
squat on the bar so the patron could have his turn petting the
wild pony. This might've gone on for a minute or two or
three, but then it was over before anything ever erupted from
anywhere. A buck a fondle. Pretty good prices, I had to admit.
You could do a lot worse, and believe me, I have. A friend of
mine was so intrigued with this place that she interviewed

some of the dancers. She found out that there were strict rules stating that the dancers would be fired on the spot if they ejaculated. So, they told her, they would just beat off maybe four times in a row before coming to work. You know, it goes along with the job. I later found out that an ordinance in D.C. did outlaw opposite-sex touching in clubs, but this ordinance was written before anyone thought about same-sex touching. I mean, I'm sure some people were thinking about it, but probably not the people making the ordinances.

The night was a complete success as far as I was concerned. Where else can a girl go to listen to great music, be surrounded by men, get to stare at numerous penises without anyone caring, and see possibly the longest specimen on the face of the earth? Then we fought our way to the door to check out a drag show next door, where a tall, manly man was doing a paltry imitation of Donna Summer singing "Bad girl, bad girl, you're such a dirty bad girl, beep beep."

This night was a perfect illustration of my point. Given the right situation (a relaxed and friendly atmosphere, whether it be with all men, a man and a woman, or any of a multitude of combinations), when men are completely relaxed, uninhibited, and unencumbered by fears of judgment, the penis is usually the focal point of the evening, whether you are a three-year-old running around naked, a man romancing a woman, or a naked dancer with balm in his socks. With a built-in stick shift there for your own personal driving pleasure from day 1, is it any wonder men think the way they do? I'm not saying that it is really justifiable that they are the ones who make the mess and we are the ones who usually have to get up and get the Kleenex, just suddenly understandable how they come into the world with a sense of penile entitlement.

So now you understand how they got to be the way they are. In the thrust and parry of the romantic duel, it is always best to know as much as you can about your opponent. Not that it will smooth your ride in any way; you can forget that, sister, for you are on one bumpy road. But the more knowledge you can gather, the better chance you have of beating them at their own game, which is, of course, the objective. To your already extensive, far-reaching database, I will add the little nuggets and pearls of wisdom I have come to gather over the years, and if we all team up and pool our resources, then maybe there is hope for the sexes to get along, the species to propagate, and civilization as we know it to continue. But I doubt it.

BAD BOYS, FLINGS, AND STATE REPRESENTATIVES

A girl can wait for the right man to come along but in the meantime that still doesn't mean she can't have a wonderful time with all the wrong ones.

—CHER

EVERYONE HAS TO HAVE their flings. A fling is not to be confused with a boyfriend or a potentially serious relationship. It could always grow *into* the real thing, but honey, don't get your hopes up. Flings are a category in and of themselves. And they are not to be confused with affairs. Affairs are the flings that you have when you are married, a whole different moral matter. I don't know one married person who has not considered an affair at some time or another, so let's just categorize that as another thing that everyone wonders about, most people fantasize about, and some people do. More than one married friend has called me on the phone, sworn me to secrecy, and confessed that she is not just attracted to another man but is all but gouging out her own eyes and lopping off her hands to prevent herself from acting on it. This seems normal to me. It is the circumstances in which people cross the line that are always unpredictable, and shocking once you find out. Mr. Brown, the next-door neighbor, who walks his dog every morning, kisses his wife good-bye, and then goes to the office where he writes motivational books about how to be a good husband, complete with useful tips on how to keep a marriage alive? An insatiable adulterer. Ms. Lehman, the family friend who's been married forty years and raised seven bright, upstanding children? A secret bigamist. One of my girlfriends, whom I would vote least likely to have an affair with a married man, had one. Who would've thunk? I've known affairs that have blown apart not just families but whole communities, in fact nations, for that matter. The bad thing about affairs is that there is so much at risk—precisely, I'm sure, why some people enter into them.

Flings, on the other hand, are basically free of charge. Not being legally bound to another person, one is free to fling at will, and as long as one flings responsibly, I say could there be anything better? All the thrill of an affair without the home wrecking, the ostracism, or those pesky scheduling conflicts. In a fling, the only thing you risk is your mental health, to which I say, that's why God created therapists. Forward, march.

A fling is quite delicious, at least for the first week or so. If it ends there, you may walk away with some of your mental faculties intact. If it goes on much longer than that, well, then it runs the risk of turning into a *relationship*, to which I say, duck and cover. New flings are like coming home to a great big package on your doorstep; it could be something great for which you've waited a long time, it could be a surprise so shocking that it knocks the wind right out of you, or it could be a bomb that scars you for life (or kills you slowly and agonizingly). Of course, the great beauty of a fling is that one never knows just how it will turn out. And it is the great mystery therein that keeps our blood flowing, our hearts pumping, our stomachs churning.

The other great beauty of a fling is that you don't have to be constrained by the standards you would normally hold a potential boyfriend up to. No, the very definition of a fling is that the object of your desire doesn't have to meet all your everyday requirements. Just one of them is enough. And of course this opens up the possibilities to include such luminaries as the copyboy at work, the guy you always flirt with at the video store, and the sherpa you met on your last trip to Nepal.

Which is not to say that you shouldn't have at least some expectations. Some standards are required for a good fling, even if they exist solely for you to ball up and toss over your shoulder as you take the arm of your newest conquest. The sheer sense of possibility involved in having a fling is such sweet torture, such an excruciating source of excitement, that nothing else quite compares. What could be more exciting than the adorable way he never calls you back? The bewitching way he keeps floating back to old girlfriends? The irresistible way he encourages you to see other men? A veritable treasure trove of memories.

A fling is not a pastime for the faint of heart, the meek, the girl who sleeps better with someone than without. It is for the bold and fearless, the adventuress who understands deep in her wild heart that this is life's greatest roller coaster and then boldly buys a lifelong ticket (okay, maybe not lifelong, but at least until she's married or committed).

My primary fling interests, like those of many women of worth, were always the Bad Boys. Now, a bad boy to someone else may be defined as someone who has done jail time, drives a Harley, and picks his fingernails with a machete. But I define the bad boy a little differently. To me a bad boy can be anyone who is *all wrong for you* for any of a thousand reasons. In my case, he has a razor-sharp sense of humor, a streak of real creative genius (so far so good), and a deep-seated insecurity that can be perfectly repaired by a girl like me (the clincher!). What I have come to learn over the years, however, is that generally, my own personal bad boys have two strikes against them. One is that the deep-seated insecurities are usually the tip of a great big insecurity iceberg, and while this dark side is wildly attractive to me for years on end, I eventually end up playing the role of the *Titanic*. The second is that bad boys are attracted to either bad girls or Betty Crockers, not quirky Jewish girls who still tear up when they unexpectedly hear Carole King on the radio. Trying to snare a bad boy is like losing those last five pounds. It's a constant exercise in frustration, but you're compelled to try anyway. It's hard for any self-respecting girl to walk away from a challenge that great. For me, it was impossible.

Of course, bad boys are also unpredictable and develop a chameleon-like survival skill. They are therefore likely to transform into any number of people, depending on what they want from you. They have a whole repertoire of men within: the one who regales you with tales of his rebellion, the one who feels bad about his past and wants you to help him reform, the one who takes you along on his wild antics until you realize that you haven't slept for days and there is an all-points bulletin with your name on it that would really upset your mom if she found out, the one who entertains you constantly and avoids all matters serious, the one who is on a rocket ride and wants you to hold on to the tailpipe, and the one whose life is just a plain train wreck and invites you to steer.

But, as we have established, the true thrill of a fling is that you are not limited by your usual tastes. This is where you can stretch out, go out on a limb, see how other gals live. Whereas you are usually a sensible girl and go out mostly with mature men with stable jobs, their own apartments, and a savings account, here is your chance to contribute to the delinquency of a minor, date a Republican, or make it with the Maytag repairman just because you adore the way he looks in a standard-issue prisonlike jumpsuit.

Flings with bad boys are particularly pointed reminders that at any moment one thing may appeal to you and at another moment your desires could be completely different. That is what flings are for, changes in the weather of your psychological landscape. The sherpa of today may be the reject of tomorrow, and the reject of tomorrow may transform overnight, like the ninety-pound weakling who gets sand kicked in his face, into the bully of your dreams. For the bad boy is not known for his overall appeal and his well-rounded qualities. He is best loved for one very specific quality that he has in spades over the guys who are well-rounded perfect catches. For instance, he is a miserable person with no integrity and the loyalty of a praying mantis, but he is funny as hell. Or maybe he is just smart as hell. Or maybe he has great forearms, does great accents, or makes a mean chicken cacciatore. He could merely have one crooked tooth where you like crooked teeth, and you are putty in his hands. So we know in our rational minds that these boys have no future with us if we are serious about actual quality, but in the face of a quality that you have a weakness for and he has an abundance of, well, we can expect only so much of ourselves, can we not?

I knew one bad boy whose life was just a constant stream of brilliant fuck-ups. Wouldn't that fact alone be enough to make you want to jump his bones? It was for me. He just couldn't help himself from destroying everyone he came near, in a loving kind of way. And everyone wanted to be near him. He had a magnetism that could charm a tequila worm back to life. Funny, smart, creative, manic, and best of all, dangerous. Not dangerous in that he might hurt you or that you would become a scofflaw if you hung out with him. He was *emotionally* dangerous, the most magnetic of all bad-boy qualities. And me being the brilliant armchair psychologist, we were obviously the perfect couple. You just knew, if you rode on his coattails, you would end up having the adventure of a lifetime, provided you lived to tell about it.

And while I was immediately set aflame upon meeting this man, whom we shall call Tweedledee, and rightously imagined myself to be the one woman who could tame the wild boar, he did not look at me as such. In fact, he started dating one of my best friends. And ironically, I started dating one of his. This was not in any way calculated or spiteful on my part or on hers, since she was unaware that at the time I thought he was the bee's knees. And when they started dating, this closed off all possibility of my own romantic link with the guy, which was fine with me, since my loyalty to her was far greater than my crush on him. Okay, so I still had a crush on him, but you know, no biggie. I was engrossed in a blast-off stage of my own with his friend, whom we shall call Tweedledum. Why not?

Now, Tweedledum was, in his own right, a fascinating guy. And also emotionally dangerous. Beautiful, isn't it? He was the kind of guy that all woman fall for at some time or another, because he was a talker. He knew his way around the human psyche, proving himself to be as female as you can get and still be a guy—and I mean that as the highest compliment. When T. Dum asked me out I was completely thrilled. Intimidated even. He was an original thinker and clever and smart. Enough to make me want to feign laryngitis so that I didn't have to compete (and I am not easily intimidated in the art of verbal exchange). He could laugh at himself. He could laugh at everyone else. And when he poured attention on you, it was like a laser beam, hot and intense. He literally made you feel like the bomb could drop right next to you and he would force it to wait until you had finished what you had to say before allowing it to explode. In fact, it was almost embarrassing. I wasn't exactly used to being stared at like I was Ginger to his Gilligan. But this is something a girl could get used to.

I felt we were in sync, even though I suffered waves of self-doubt. On one of our first dates, we were walking down the street talking about books and movies. The discussion landed on the film *Broadcast News,* still one of my favorites. I casually said to him, "You know what the best line in that movie was?" and he said, like he was reading a cue card in my head, " 'Okay, so I buried the lead,' " and I screamed, "*Yes! Yes!* Exactly!" and jumped up and down with excitement as though this was proof positive that we were going to ride off into the sunset with a beautiful future, a golden retriever, and a big, fat trust fund.

However, it was only a matter of weeks before he dropped me like a hot potato. I have no idea why. Upon questioning he just mumbled something about not being in a good place right now. I will mention here that he was in a good enough place to fall deeply, madly, and wildly in love with someone famous shortly thereafter. But before he did, his friend Tweedledee entered the picture one more time. T. Dee was about to leave the country, and, as we had established a friendship, I called him to wish him a fond farewell and left a message asking him to call back before he left if he had a chance. He called back at midnight one night when both my good friend and T. Dum were conveniently out of town, and told me he was coming over to say good-bye. I thought this was exactly the kind of fun, adventurous, against-your-better-judgment kind of thing that was so great about this guy. Coming over at the spur of the moment at one A.M. (while, as it happened, I had a girlfriend visiting from home who was sleeping soundly in my bedroom).

Was I thinking that men come over to women's houses in the middle of the night while their girlfriends are away after having had a few drinks for a little light conversation? For some goofing around? Flirting in that we-won't-do-anything-but-it's-fun-to-pretend-we-would kind of way? Exactly! *Exactly* what I was thinking. Okay, so I was a little naive. It was a long time ago. So when, after a few minutes of joking around, he went to kiss me, I recoiled. Under normal circumstances I would never have recoiled, but my loyalty to my friend, his girlfriend, plagued me greatly.

"What about Sarah? What about Tweedledum? Don't you think this is just a little too weird?"

And this was his absolutely beautiful bad-boy response:

"I am about to leave the country for a war-torn land. I am on a whole different *plane* of weirdness." Translation: Forget about your concerns, they are minor compared to the upheaval and mental morass that is *my* life. Seize the moment and let me slip my hand up your shirt. And while I didn't kick him out onto the street right then and there, even though I should have, I was semimature enough to recognize the situation for the bomb that it was and left it alone to the best of my ability. He slept it off on the floor of my living room and left at six o'clock the next morning.

Tweedledee was famous for his indiscretions, flirtations, sexual harassments, affairs, and flings. And he usually got away with it because he had the perfect mixture of bad-boy-ness (emotionally wild and unpredictable, to say nothing of totally unreliable) with smarts and intrigue. The man was a walking demolition crew. Completely alluring.

In other words, the perfect bad boy. Known to be a romantic time bomb, he lures you in despite all your better judgment and then, true to promise, blows your heart to smithereens. Like he did to about a thousand women. After this episode and the postscript of watching him wantonly mistreat my friend, I stopped talking to him altogether, despite the fact that he is now rich and famous and extremely well connected. (Am I mature, or what? And, I might mention, Tweedledum is well on his way.) This guy was addicted to excitement and seemingly indifferent to the bodies left in his wake. And if you're just a (semi) normal kind of gal, the excitement addict can be too much to resist, even though you know that he is about as good for you as mixing sleeping pills with alcohol.

Then there are the boys who defy categorization. Like one bad-boy fling who turned out to be such a good boy, he was like a fortress of virtue. In this particular case, it wasn't that he was wild or dangerous, but there was just something about him that drove me to distraction. It turned out to be the sheer magnitude of his kick-ass confidence. The kind of thing that would lead an exchange such as this:

ME: "You know something, you are a real asshole."
HIM: "But I am the *best* asshole you know."

I had to agree. And once a girl is hooked on this fling's *je ne sais quoi*, it could take wild horses, decades of therapy, or years of brutal rejections to kick the habit.

This one began in a greasy spoon where I slung hash and served up Velveeta nachos. The man in question was one of my coworkers. Blond, muscular, big smile, square teeth, easy laugh. Not necessarily conventionally handsome, but mighty attractive nonetheless. Many of my female coworkers had crushes on him. Whereas this sort of competition may squelch the desire in some women, it wasn't a problem for me; in fact, it was an added plus. If you can win over so many other competitors, is not the victory that much sweeter? He also happened to have a long-standing girlfriend, which most people found to be a deterrent. I saw it as incentive. Because he went on to become a public figure, making me something of his Gennifer Flowers, I cannot use his real name. So, I will call him . . . Shmo. Why not?

Shmo had confidence the likes of no one I have known before or since. He attacked life as though things would always go his way, and sure enough, they did. It was a quality you could easily hate him for, but I found his cockiness downright magnetic. I was drawn to him like a lemming to the sea and, as it turned out, with the same ultimate outcome. And I was not the only one. He sweated charisma. I was undeterred by his longtime girlfriend for three reasons. First, her name was Kelly. Okay? Please. Second, she was mousy and boring and so nice it was sickening, and I found it very hard to believe he could prefer a boring life with her to a wildly scintillating life with me. Third, he rarely mentioned her and spent more time with me. So far, so good.

Our relationship began to thicken outside of work when we would take your typical getting-to-know-you long walks in the wee hours and talk for hours about, you know, the universe and everything in it. People began to wonder what was going on, me included. But it was early yet, and I, being a little short in the self-preservation department, thought that the slow progression was somehow directly related to the quality of the future relationship. The more we talked and spent time together, the more fascinating he became to me. He was smart and funny and beautiful and he was pouring a lot of his abundant energy my way. What was not to like? Everyone knew that he was quite a catch, and it was fast looking like I had the best lure. So imagine my complete and utter surprise when, on one of our long and typically soul-searching early-relationship walks, he said something that stopped me dead in my tracks. And I mean Dead. In one instant he threw me into a state of shock so great I was dumbfounded and speechless and racking my brain as to how I could have totally, totally missed the boat on this one. He started telling me about the Lord.

The Lord! Dear God, he might as well have told me that he'd been abducted by aliens and taken away to the mother ship, which, if you look at it from my point of view, is pretty much the same thing. I was completely thrown off. Now, I have to explain here that while I was brought up in a Jewish home, with candle lighting, temple outings, Bat Mitzvahs, and the works, it wasn't exactly a religious household. I personally am not really very big on the whole God thing. Not that I don't believe in a certain spirituality and miraculousness to the world, but you know, I just don't see it as the doing of a big guy in a gray beard who knows about everything that is going to happen to everyone everywhere, whose son died for our sins. What can I say? I wish I did. I mean, I think life would be a whole lot easier if I could just take my troubles and lay them at the feet of Jesus and forget about them. If I didn't have to answer life's traumatic and troubling questions for myself, because think of the money I could save on antidepressants. But it's just not in me. I am too practical for faith. If I can't see it, hear it, taste it, smell it, or touch it, forget it. I respect your right to believe, but please, don't try to bring me into the fold; that's where I have to draw the line.

After my initial shock, I had an unlikely reaction to his revelation: I saw it as perhaps my single greatest challenge yet. Because I knew, like so many who'd come before, that his was a problem that could be repaired by only one woman, me. He was the One, if I could only talk him out of this God thing. While he started out as fling material, I now wanted to move him along into the relationship category, especially since it looked so difficult (and because it looked so difficult, a fling would be the perfect compromise. In other words, I would've been happy either way). At the same time, I think the wheels in his head were starting to turn the same way; I could be the One if only I *believed*. It was a perfect denouement in the works. Too bad I wasn't a member of Jews for Jesus. We would've made a perfect couple. I should mention that while at the time I met him he had voted for Jimmy Carter and sported an earring, this was a short blip of liberalism on his part, and he is now an arch-conservative legislator in a large midwestern state. How was I supposed to know? Can I help it if our paths happened to cross in the single liberal moment of his life? Call it fate, call it kismet, call it unfortunate, but there it is for all to see.

And so, as time went on, we each continued to believe that we would one day achieve our goal, to persuade the other to change their stripes and live happily ever after. In the meantime, we acted like Harry and Sally. He would throw stones at my window late at night and I would come and meet him for a midnight adventure. I would go to his house at three A.M. dressed as Carmen Miranda and sit at his bedside till he felt my presence and woke up, howling with laughter, at which point we'd go have breakfast and blow off our morning classes. We gave each other surprise gifts that were carefully chosen to have special meaning, but without importance enough to call into question the frustratingly platonic nature of our relationship. We'd debate endlessly about God and Christianity and Judaism and atheism. He would smoke clove cigarettes and argue that Christianity had been bastardized and was unfortunately now the purview of TV preachers in velveteen and Brylcreem. That the real thing, the original text and all, was okay once it was all sifted through. I could buy that, I just didn't believe it. This relationship was perfectly safe because the odds of it ever working were so minuscule. Which is precisely what kept me going and allowed me to let my emotional guard down. When you are pursuing something, your guard has to be so far down you couldn't reach it if you wanted to because you are too busy pouring on the charm, and to really pour on the charm, you can't be guarded—that only comes later, after you've already established yourself as a couple. Then it's guard galore.

Eventually, it dawned on me (so very young was I) that he was spending more time with me than with sprightly little Kelly, yet she was the one with her hands in his pockets. I couldn't help but feel that I was being made a fool, or at least a simp, by way of not getting what I wanted, and though this was normally a situation I felt right at home in, even I knew it was time to raise the *question*. So, on a bright sunny day on a picnic blanket under a tree, I sucked in some air, mustered up every ounce of courage I could squeeze out, and asked him what was going on. He reiterated that she was his girlfriend and I was just someone he adored. This of course made me walk away thinking that I had the better end of the deal. I mean, girlfriends come and go all the time, but to be someone who *doesn't* come and go, someone who is *adored*, now, *that's* something.

The other thing that my experience with him illustrates perfectly is the fact that once you pass the age of maybe eighteen or twenty, you never have really good friendships with members of the opposite sex unless there are copious amounts of sexual tension roiling away under the surface. It's true. You may have to dig hard to find it, and you don't have to act on it, but to deny this truth is like saying you caught Martha Stewart in white after Labor Day. Unfortunately, there are those of us who take a good twenty-five years or so to figure this out, and I would be right at the head of that pack.

But there it was, staring me in the face: He had a girlfriend, and I was just a really, *really* good friend. Prized and cherished. Fuck you. What made this situation even more frustrating was that I was wildly attracted to him—as much as you can be to someone who thinks you will probably burn in hell for all of eternity. But alas, this mismatch was not meant to be. For a while.

Two years later, long after we'd both graduated and were on our way to we had no idea where, he was teaching in the (aptly named) Virgin Islands, and though we kept in loose touch, I hadn't talked to him in some time. Enough time to have had real boyfriends and a few flings. I called him on a lark. He said that he and Kelly had broken up (could she have been too boring even for him?), airfares were cheap, and I should make a few calls. I called him back and said, "What are you doing this weekend?" Had I forgotten that he loved the Lord? No, I was just ignoring it, as any girl in her right mind would in the face of an invitation to the Virgin Islands from a beautiful man she'd had a crush on for three years. Even if I couldn't convert that old boy, I was ready for the fling of a lifetime.

It was February. I was in Chicago. Need I say more? I left home and crept through the snow at four in the morning in nothing but a flimsy skirt (my sister's), flimsier blouse (my sister's), and a pair of sandals, toting my straw hat and sunscreen behind me. This was clearly a make-it-or-break-it situation for which I wanted to be properly clad. Obviously, I was betting on the former. Every girl should experience this kind of thing once in her life. It's like going to the doctor and being told you need to gain weight. I don't mean going out with a born-again who wants to save himself until marriage, I'm talking about having the kind of fling that is quintessentially picturesque, similar to living in the backdrop of a sickeningly sappy postcard. It's good for the soul. When I got off the plane, I was welcomed by crystal-clear skies, flowers the size of my head, pristine blue-green water, sparkling white sand, and a man running to meet me who actually picked me up and twirled me around like we'd been cast in *Love Story* on the Caribbean. We started acting out a Barbara Cartland novel. The electricity in the air was so palpable that I can still remember the tiniest of details despite the fact that it was fifteen years ago. The taste of the burgers he grilled, what I wore, what he said, what was playing on the radio, you know, that kind of thing. And as we sat on the beach under stars that looked like the cover of a Harlequin romance, we inched closer and closer together and, finally, he kissed me. Then he looked at me intensely and said, right on cue, "I've been wanting to do that for years."

Of course, at this point it took every ounce of self-control not to slap him upside his head and yell, "Well, for Christ's sake, you idiot, why didn't you? I did everything but put a bull's-eye in my crotch, what are you, *blind*?" But instead I just said demurely, "You should have."

For three days, we played and played, getting up in the middle of the night to feed each other oranges, listening to the rain every morning while entwined in crisp white sheets, and frolicking in our own little personal paradise. I felt like I was living in a sappy dream, and of course someone as brilliant as yourself has already figured out that I was. I actually found myself getting a little more religious as I started praying that he wouldn't bring up the subject of God. I figured it this way: I was young and I wanted nothing more than to burrow into him as far as I could. I knew we had our differences, and I was perfectly willing to put them aside and soak this opportunity for all it was worth. I didn't think anyone should get in the way of my happiness, least of all God. But he was an iron man, and on day number four I could feel the blow coming. And trust me, it wasn't the one I wanted. As I sat there in his robe, he explained it all to me.

"I can't marry someone who doesn't share the most important thing in my life," he said.

I was stunned. Marry? I thought. Marry?! Who said anything about getting married? Couldn't we just do the hoochy-coo and forget the Big Guy for a while? But instead I was calm and begged him to ignore the petty differences between us and look at the fun we could have together. He stuck to his guns. I brought out my full artillery. I argued and cajoled, reasoned and explained that we were young; this was the time to explore other worlds; we loved to be together; for Christ's sake, lighten *up*! We were in a standoff. Which, I might add, filled the next three days of my vacation with not doing what I'd come there to do. Instead we talked about anything that had anything to do with anything, as long as it had nothing to do with him and me—many resisted impulses on my part, many feelings of righteousness on his. Even after I got on a plane back to the frozen tundra of the Midwest, I was blind to the writing on the wall and proceeded to obsess about him for months anyway. A smart girl like yourself will understand just what a sorry state I was in when I tell you that part of me was actually flattered by this whole thing. I mean, he had me in the *marrying* category. So what if that meant no more nookie, I still saw it, albeit delusionally, as a real compliment. What can I say? Everyone has to have a few dark episodes that make her the fine, upstanding, and well-balanced person she is today.

We flirted around for a few more months after he got home, but it was clear that he was moving forward and I was sort of hanging onto his leg as he tried to walk away. He met his future wife soon afterward, and I went on to have a few thousand more episodes like this. Every once in a while I still get a call from my mother or one of my girlfriends telling me that they saw his face on a billboard or that he was up for reelection or that he was introducing some arch-conservative bill into the state legislature. Now, as it turns out, he is running for the U.S. House of Representatives, and by the time I'm fifty, he will probably be the vice-presidential candidate while I am sending away for Miracle Stretch Mark Cream.

The irony of the whole thing, despite my years of wizened maturity, well-honed experience, and certain self-confidence, is the fact that while we probably have about as much in common now as Lucifer and the pope, if he walked into the room right now, my pulse would still start racing. My heart would do a back flip and I would start sweating in places where no sweat glands exist. I would probably laugh a little too hard, talk a little too loud, and find myself inadvertently doing something like twirling my hair.

This is the irony of a once-longed-for guy. The crush never goes away. Especially if it is unrequited or unconsummated or otherwise unfinished. In this case, the question of what might have been starts eating away at a girl's resolve, and that is when curiosity has the potential of getting the better of her. Of course, there is one sure remedy to this situation: Spend a little time with your old beloved and you will fast find out what split you up in the first place. This is why broken-up couples and divorcées sleep with their exes at least once. After you break up, the stuff you hated about him eventually recedes and the part you liked comes to the forefront. You start feeling reminiscent and sentimental. After you get back together, it's just the opposite. Rest assured it won't be long until he does something that reminds you how much you hate him, but in that small window of opportunity, many a vow has been broken. But I have found that if you bash your head against the wall enough times, you can't help but wise up to the likely outcome: a spiral downward like a plummeting meteor. But if you're as demented a thrill seeker as I am, then the ride up is always worth the fall.

As it happens, almost all my flings have been with men I have worked with. There is a perfect explanation for this phenomenon. When you are on a date with someone, your radar is sharply focused. Your brain is like a computer, constantly evaluating the situation for future potential. Do you think that the velour top he's wearing is truly representative of his wardrobe, or is this an anomaly that he happened to grab because he was in such a hurry after performing that last brain surgery? Does he chew like that all the time or is he just getting over a busted jaw he received while defending a lost child from a group of hoodlums? Could you really see yourself with someone who has a Neil Sedaka collection, or is he just a savvy businessman who knows that it might be worth something someday to someone who is nothing like him? On a date, a man doesn't stand a chance. The whole dog-and-pony show is set up so that you sit in judgment like the goddess you are while he tries to explain away his days as a mime in the seventies. Or vice versa. You know it has gone too far when the evening is drawing to an awkward close and one of you exclaims, "But wait! You haven't seen me tap-dance yet!"

But your biggest hope for a coworker is merely that you don't despise him. That he doesn't have any really annoying habits like eating cream of broccoli soup with his hands (not fingers, mind you—hands, as in scooping it out and inserting it into his mouth—as one of my coworkers did. He was blind, but still, how gauche). You have no expectations of your coworkers as potential dates, and as any underdog team will tell you, beautiful things can happen when there is no pressure to perform. You could actually find yourself with a sudden fondness for velour or a yen to hear Neil Sedaka. Things creep up on you at work. You are pretty much able to act normally—as is he—so he no longer has to be Hercules for you to notice him. And if you have to work closely with someone on an intense project, well, there is pretty much no way to avoid the fact that you will want to jump his bones at some point. You may or may not actually do it, but rest assured, you will surely want to. And even if you don't want to consciously, then you will wake up in the middle of the night saying to yourself, "Did I just have a whipped-cream dream about . . . Mr. Johnson?" In the commonality of working on the same thing at an intense pitch, lines begin to blur, and your togetherness on one front begets togetherness on another. It is as reliable as the sorry aftermath to follow.

For unless one of you is a short-term employee, or maybe you live in different cities, it is the rare exception that goes from workplace affair to stable relationship. Mostly they self-destruct for all to see by the water fountain, in the parking lot, in the conference room, or in an editing booth. And there is nothing worse than having to walk around your workplace on eggshells, avoiding the icy stares of the man you just dumped overboard. The workplace fling must be carefully analyzed for potential ways in which it could ruin your life forever. However, there are times when analysis must be left to the people

holed up in libraries writing their dissertations on the work-
ings of the Cray computer, and the jumping ahead blindly
must be left to brazen girls such as yourself.

Conferences, of course (as anyone who has ever been to
one will tell you), provide one of the most fertile playing fields
for flings. If you happen to be working on an intense project
with someone that culminates in a conference, well, you are
pretty much a goner, unless you have the will of Arnold
Schwarzenegger and the beliefs of an arch-conservative legislator in a large midwestern state. Having no such beliefs, I
packed my bags with gusto.

The man I'd been working with on the intense aforementioned sexual-tension-producing project was someone I still
have the highest regard for, particularly since he wanted to
sleep with me. His appeal was his verbal acuity, his quick wit,
and his wide breadth of knowledge. The more I got to know
him, the more he made me laugh, and the more attractive the
space between his front teeth became. Being around him
sharpened my own wit, and together our repartee was a
strong aphrodisiac. William Powell and Myrna Loy had nothing on us. Hepburn and Tracy? Amateurs. Who could resist
such a dynamic? No way. It was predestined, written in the
sand. It was a must.

And so it was that we found ourselves at a conference full
of important people in our field, two of whom were sharing
his room. We were lollygagging around in the pool on the
roof of the hotel, flirting with abandon, when we realized that
we were surrounded by station managers and program direc-
tors and people who probably didn't need to bear witness to
our adolescent antics. So we decided to retire to the comforts
of his room. Specifically, the shower. It was a long shower.

And as we sat in our towels, he at the sink and me on the counter, exchanging soggy but still witty remarks, we were completely unprepared for what came next.

A knock on the door. It was followed by the brisk entrance of one of his roommates, Very Important Person in the Field Number One. He immediately shut the door. I was instantly covered with misty sweat.

"Hello?" my coworker called out.

"Hello?" said Very Important Person Number One. "What are you up to?"

"Just . . . taking a shower," he said through the closed door. "What are *you* doing?"

"I thought I'd take a little break, maybe rest for a while."

I glared at my soaking friend. Mouthing words to him as though he didn't understand English. "You . . . have . . . got . . . to . . . get . . . me . . . out . . . of . . . here!"

He nodded and motioned for me to step into the tub, in my towel, while he closed the shower curtain. This is when I wanted to wring my own neck. All of a sudden I was an X-rated Lucy Ricardo. What the hell was I doing standing naked in a towel in a bathtub with the curtain drawn, other than praying to a deity I didn't believe in? I felt like I was re-creating a really bad episode of *Love, American Style,* truer than the red, white, and blue—ooh-ooh-ooh, love, American style, that's me and you. I was an updated Gidget to his Moondog. He left the bathroom, leaving the door open a crack.

I could hear their chitchat while my friend, I'll call him Shnook, said things like "So, how's the conference going?" to which the important person in the field would say, "You know, same as always. You seen one totebag, you've seen 'em all." At which point Shnook would say, "Let's go down to the lounge and I'll buy you a drink," and "Gorgeous day outside, isn't it? We should get out and enjoy it."

Here is where I had to start wondering just what I would do, in a towel behind the shower curtain, if Very Important Person in the Field Number One came into his hotel bathroom to use the toilet or God knows what else—and I felt a sneeze coming on. I started rocking like a baby. Suddenly I heard Shnook say with great enthusiasm, "I have to use the bathroom!"

He came in and, without so much as a glance, threw my clothes, which were strewn about the room, into the bathtub. "Your *clothes*," he whispered, as though I had purposely left them on the floor like a flashing neon sign saying FIRE ME, FIRE ME as he unzipped his fly to pee.

"Well," I whispered back, "it's not like I was expecting company. You have *got* to get rid of him!"

"I am *trying*!" he exclaimed as he flushed.

He left the room and renewed his conversation with Very Important Person in the Field Number One.

That is, until Very Important Person in the Field Number Two put his key into the lock and joined the party. I could hear Shnook greeting him a little too loudly, as if to send a signal my way. I looked up and started counting the tiles on the side of the tub. Who knew they were made in Jersey? The things you learn when time is on your side.

"So, how 'bout that drink?" Shnook was saying loudly. They were gathering consensus when yet again, there was a knock on the door.

"Housekeeping!" said a muffled female voice.

"Can you come back a little bit later?" Shnook said quickly, before anyone else could think.

So far there were 183 tiles to my right. I started wondering if I really wanted to work in radio after all. I briefly considered stenography, then went back to counting tiles. I was up to 312 when I heard—could it possibly be?—*another* knock on the door. Only this time it was the door that adjoined their room to my room—ironically, we were in adjoining suites. And I was sharing that adjoining room with my boss, Karen, who, as it happened, was knocking at the door. I heard ol' Shnook open the suite door.

"Have you seen Gwen?"

"I think she went out for a Coke," he riffed. I felt like Dorothy when the wicked witch locked her in the room with nothing but a bleeding hourglass and a crystal ball. In the crystal ball Dorothy could see Auntie Em pleading, "Dorothy? Dorothy? Where are you, Dorothy?" And Dorothy was shouting, "Here I am, I'm here! I'm trapped in an awful place and I'm never going to get out! Oh, Auntie *Em!*" I wanted to shout out to my boss, "I'm here. Here! Behind the curtain! I'm the one with the goose bumps and the raisin skin. Help me, please!" But just as the last grain of sand slipped through the hourglass, I heard the suite door closing.

"Oh," said my boss. "Okay. If you see her, tell her I'm looking for her." And with that she closed the door, dashing all my hopes of rescue.

The conversation in the room resumed among the Important Persons in the Field as Shnook tried desperately (without appearing desperate) to usher them out the door. Then he hit upon something that was sheer and utter brilliance on his part. A surefire way to rid a room of men faster than a hand grenade.

"Well, how 'bout we go down to the bar and watch the game?" he asked them.

You see, it doesn't really matter what season of year it was, what city we were in, what time of day it was, or anything else. Gather three men in a room and give them the option to "watch the game" versus sitting around and talking, and they will always choose the former. What game? Who knew and who cared? It could have been the World Curling Championships, and men would still be more interested in watching it than having any kind of meaningful conversation. I have never been more grateful for universally Neanderthal male qualities. As they straggled out of the room, I listened desperately for the click of the lock to close. Before they had turned the hall corner, I was dressed and peeking out the door to see if the coast was clear. As soon as they were out of eyesight, I went tearing out of the room, around the corner, and knocked on the door to our room. There stood my boss.

"Where were you?" Karen asked.

"Shmoozing. You know conferences. Want to get a Coke?"

"I thought you just got one."

"I, uh, forgot my money. That's right. See? No pockets," I added. "We could go down to the lobby and have a drink," I found myself saying.

"There's a Coke machine down the hall." Coke had never played such a singularly important role in my life.

"Yeah, but I don't want to sit in the room on such a nice day," I said, hoping that she would not say the obvious: "Oh, and the darkened hotel lobby is so bright and airy!"

"Okay," she agreed. God bless her agreeability. We went down to the hotel lobby. And of course who should we see there but two Very Important People in Radio. And Shnook. We went and joined them.

"Thirsty?" I said, looking right at Shnook.

"You know," he said, "suddenly I am. I must have burned off more at this conference than I thought."

Within an hour, he had to fly back to his home city, many hours away from where I was living. His leave-taking was very quick, which was as it should've been. He ran up to pack his bags and had to run out the door to catch his plane. No time for false promises of writing or calling, particularly since one of us (not me) was already involved with someone else. It was fast and clean, no time for festering. Within two days I had confessed my trespass to Karen over a room-service sundae at two A.M. A girl cannot keep an episode like that a total secret. Like Augustus Gloop, she's likely to explode. Besides, this boss was one of my closest girlfriends, and I knew that as such she would take my secret to her grave. And so, whereas I saw Shnook once or twice after that, our witty repartee-induced sexual tension was, for the most part, left dripping on the bathroom floor like the towels we dropped in the commotion. If I saw him again, I'm sure there would be a small spark of some kind, but the moment passed long ago. If you're lucky, flings present themselves at just the right moment when both of you are in the exact same place and the atmospheric pressure is just right. Then a fling is a beautiful thing. And for a chance at that, a girl has to be ready for anything. Even dating.

DATING, SHMATING

How many of you started dating someone because you were too lazy to commit suicide?

—Judy Tenuta

DATING.

What's the point?

I am here to tell you exactly what the point is. First off (what most people think of as the real point of dating), the point is to let yourself fall wildly for someone who catches your fancy in one way or another and suspend all semblance of reality, which allows you to enjoy a time period ranging from about a week to a year or more of total infatuation and stomach-churning giddiness. This is the equivalent of dating colostrum. What people call liquid gold. The really good stuff. The stuff that people label as falling in love, the stuff that people look back to as the great times of yesteryear, the goo that makes you soar high, high, high. And it is this adrenaline rush, this love-sick no-eating-no-sleeping obsession that fuels us to live through the moment when we find out that our beloved has a secret shrine to Marie Osmond and in her honor wears a sheer lace teddy under his clothes at all times. We are disappointed, yes, but eventually someone else comes along who takes us on a rocket ride and we are fueled for another month, year, or decade.

This is where the second part comes in. The repetitive process of getting that high is an addiction that is mighty hard for a girl to break, because it is somehow hardwired into our brains to think that one day we will find the person with whom *that high never goes away*. Does the word "delusional" mean anything to you? And so the real point of dating, to a savvy girl like yourself, is to *try* and prove to yourself, over and over again, that your fantasy really does exist somewhere in the world, even if this present shlub isn't it. After all, if anyone is going to wind up with the perfect man for herself, it is going to be you, and you, being the aggressive, take-charge, no-nonsense kind of woman that you are, will find him, even if it takes dating every man on the planet—which, by the way, it does.

You see, this is the whole fallacy of dating, that the person you dream of actually exists, which, by the way, he doesn't. And even if he did, and you met him, you would be too intimidated to think yourself worthy. Think about it. What if the most attractive man you could dream of, say a George Clooney or Harrison Ford type who also happened to be witty, insightful, empathic, athletic, smart, easygoing, neat, fond of children, able to match a coat and tie, adventuresome, surprising, ambitious but valuing family life, secure, a Renaissance man, called you on your shit but understood your every neurosis and put up with your every mood? You'd be saying to yourself, I'm too fat, too lazy, too neurotic, and besides that, I pick my lips. It would be a nightmare of self-flagellation.

But the thrill of the hunt, the jubilation of those initial hyperdates is so incredible that they feed the flames of the fallacy that somewhere, with the right person, it will always be like this, which, by the way, it won't. I mean, for example, if the reason that the flame went out with guy number one was because he was so, say, immature, then you figure surely there is someone out there with all this guy's qualities who *is* mature, so you break up with guy number one and hunt for guy number two, who is mature, but, as you later find out, happens to be as boring as melba toast, so what good is he? The next guy is exciting, but stupid. The next, smart, but egotistical. And on and on and on.

Then you wake up and think, I know what the problem is! It's not that the perfect man doesn't exist, I know that the perfect man doesn't exist because I am a smart woman who's been around the block (even though I secretly hope he does and I look at other couples and think, see, she got the only living one left and it could have been me!). The real problem (as I have been told by numerous clingy, boring guys I have rejected for a variety of reasons) is that I have a problem with commitment! That's it—if I just get rid of my problem with commitment, everything will be fine and I will ride away into the sunset on a white steed led by a young and brooding Al Pacino.

So, you pay to see a therapist and work on the commitment thing, only to realize, $3,000 later (which the insurance company won't pay unless the therapist makes you sound a lot more disturbed than you are, which of course you don't want her to do in case you one day decide to run for public office, perhaps against a representative in a large midwestern state), that it isn't commitment at all that is your problem, it's reality.

Unfortunately, here's where you hit the wall, because no matter how you slice it, there's not much you can do about the real world. It's not that commitment is so hard, it's accepting the difference between what you dream of and what you get. As a wise, wise, wise friend of mine once said to me in the ladies' lounge while I was in the throes of some tumultuous breakup or ambivalent makeup, once you commit yourself to the *idea* of a relationship, you can make one work with almost *anybody*! I'm not really a person who likes to use a lot of exclamation points, but I think one is warranted here. The woman is a sage. An oracle of wisdom. Were truer words ever spoken? Genius. What you picture in your future and your relationship to the real, live, breathing person you are waking up next to who has athlete's foot (without even reaping the muscular benefits of being an athlete) are two wildly different scenarios. That is the tough part: admitting that at least one, and more likely ten or twelve or a hundred, of the attributes you think you must have, you will not get.

It's a big disappointment. A tough pill to swallow. After all, you are the exception and you deserve the exception, right? Of course you do, honey. And the good witch Glinda is coming down now in her bubble, so don't you give it a second thought. This is a problem we all suffer from, a brain split right down the middle. The right side, for instance, knows that no topical cream will reduce a thigh that is predisposed to look like a brisket. But the left side buys it anyway, and applies it generously, in a locked bathroom, late at night. The right side also knows that astrology is the equivalent of celestial three-card monte. But the left side reads all horoscopes, buys a monthly star scroll, and has an unfailing devotion to Dionne Warwick. And the right side knows that models are flukes of nature who weigh something like 30 percent less than your average American woman, but the left side is secretly contemplating rib removal for that waif waist it's always wanted.

No one ever said the brain was a rational organ. And thank God. If it were, the dreamers and schemers who have kept us marching boldly into the twenty-first century would have

thrown in the towel long ago and we would still be crossing
the prairie in a horse and buggy, which would be most unfortunate, since those *Little House on the Prairie* bonnets are just
so unbecoming.

And so, having said that, here is my own personal dating
philosophy:

I'll go out with anyone, once.

And believe me, I have. In fact, I've dated so many guys
over the years, I had to make a list. Lining up men on paper is
like creating your own personal exhibit in the museum of
romance. So what if it looks more like Diane Arbus than
Annie Leibovitz, you have a gallery all your own. Just so happens, in my case, it's the Night Gallery.

Over here on the left we have Jerry, the Quiet Man. He was
distant, with a faraway look in his eye. He sat sullenly at dinner and never uttered a word, except when the waiter suggested shrimp.

"I don't eat shrimp," he said. "It reminds me of a human
knuckle."

Here on the right is John. He lasted nine months and then
vanished, resurfacing much later to say, "Why should I call
you, just to tell you I'm not gonna call you anymore?"

Then there was Harry, who took so long to make a move
that he became the subject of our latest office pool. And who
could forget David, whose license plate said BOYCHICK, and
Andy, whom my gynecologist literally offered up while I was
wide open in the stirrups.

"I think you'll really like him. I told him *all* about you . . .
So, when was the first day of your last period?"

Guys like this are like so many used lottery tickets. Hope-
inspiring at the beginning, disappointing at the end, chance

of winning, one in twenty-six million. I'll admit that the first date can be really exciting. Until it starts. And second dates? Anyone deserves a second chance, right? But sooner or later, you have to face the Third Date. No more excuses, no more nice-nice. This is it. 'Cause let's face it, we both know you just bluffed your way through the first two. Oh, you spent the first date giving each other the Reader's Digest version of your lives, reinventing yourself in the image of Mother Teresa, Marie Curie, Aretha. On your second date, you exchanged relationship résumés, conveniently omitting that six-year period of celibacy between the one who dumped you for a world-famous author whom everyone adores and thinks is "the most refreshing talent to come along in years," and the one who still lived with his mother. Take this opportunity to rule out anyone with a monitoring device around his ankle or a waist that's smaller than yours. And now, here you are.

What makes the third date different from all other dates? The sudden, agonizing realization that you're there because you *want* to be. The stakes have gone way up. Something turns on the third date. You can no longer tell your friends that you are just going out with some guy, because this is time number three and everyone knows what that means. The time to blow him off gracefully has passed after date number two, and now you are stuck with cold sweat, dry mouth, thinly veiled mascara checks in every reflective surface you see, the works. While visions of china patterns dance through your head, sweat stains start showing through your dress guards. You are now stuck in third-date limbo. You've covered your childhood, but do you dare bring up your therapist? You've told your funniest joke, dragged him to your favorite restaurant. And besides that, you've worn your two best outfits.

The pit of your stomach is filled with that I-want-to-bear-your-children-but-what's-your-last-name? feeling, while what actually comes out of your mouth is:

"Uh . . . you've got a—you know, something stuck on the side of your mouth there . . . no, no, other side."

But hey, despite the fact that until you get married, life is just a series of relationships that don't work out, you're on your *third* date. You're sweating, and that's a good sign. Because the nature of that third date is that before the night is over, you will *know*. You will know whether you find his machine-gun laugh about as soothing as a jackhammer or whether you just go dewy eyed over the way he orders moo goo gai pan.

On the third date, you either fish or cut bait. In the act of accepting the third date alone, you are telling him that things are *possible*, and by the end of the evening, if you haven't made up your mind, you enter that surreal limbo when you have whole conversations with yourself that go like this: "Let's see, I like him well enough, but I'm not sure if I really like him well enough for any kind of commitment thing, but it gets weird after this as to why we are going out if we're not going to sleep together, but why should I sleep with someone that I've only spent a total of maybe ten hours with? On the other hand, why shouldn't I? Because if I do, he will think we are a 'thing,' and I want to leave myself an out. How did things get so complicated so fast?"

But chances are, you're having a real-live good time. You may even be envisioning the day when you let him see you unabashedly bleaching your mustache. Enjoy. Because this is the best part of any relationship. Before you really know each other. And remember, after this, you either have to live through *another* date with *another* yahoo, or step boldly into the cavernous romantic black hole so commonly referred to as the Fourth Date.

Once you are in the swing of things, hitting dates number five, eight, eleven, twelve, and thirteen, then you can settle in, hunker down for a while, watch as patterns develop that you can spend another $3,000 discussing on a therapist's couch, conveniently positioned so that you cannot see the clock as it ticks away at more than a buck and a half a minute, after you've broken up with your current *garçon du jour*. Or he's broken up with you. It didn't take long for me to determine my pattern. It went like this: Every time I knitted a guy a sweater, he'd break up with me. Of course, doing something nice for someone often results in them wanting to have nothing to do with you, so it all makes perfect sense. After a few sweaters, a girl learns her lesson. Nevertheless, sometimes things are just unpredictable. Unfortunately, unlike risky food products, men don't come with warning labels. You don't know if you're going to like it until you taste it, and if you taste it, it just may kill you. I believe in truth in advertising. I think men should sport freshness dates. That way you'd know right off the bat when they're going to spoil. When they are going to turn to you after you have just served up your best beef bourguignon (over candlelight, no less) and say things like "I'm not attracted to you anymore, I don't love you anymore, and I'm moving in with your best friend, Trixie. But we can still be friends, can't we?" You see, this way you'd know right off whether they were low in self-esteem and high in unsaturated fears, like the man who says "It's not you, it's me. I'm sort of fucked up. I'm no good for you or anyone. I think I need to spend some time getting to know myself a little better, because after all, if you can't be alone, you're no good to anyone, are you?" (One is never sure whether what he says is true and he has more baggage than Ivana Trump, or whether he is just trying to let you down easy, since you have used this very line on other men, though you hate to admit it.) With the freshness-date idea, you would know whether use of this product may be hazardous to your health or the health of your unborn children. If it is going to cause minor aches and pains, irritation, insomnia, nausea, depression, weight loss, or excessive vomiting upon hearing a line like: "You're right. I'm a jerk. I don't deserve you. You're just too good for me, and that's why I'm leaving."

You'd know whether or not you are in danger of developing a complex ("Gee, I never really thought of you in those terms. I'd hate to jeopardize our friendship. You're such a good buddy and we have so much *fun* together!") or whether you have any chance at all of at least getting to the third date.

It's enough to make a girl take a serious look in the mirror and ask herself, "Have I no breasts?"

Wake up and smell the coffee. Remember, you are in the process of getting dumped. Now is the time to hate the guy. Despise him, spread vicious rumors, and send him subscriptions to magazines that specialize in dollhouse miniatures. You clearly never want to see him again. Then, when you least expect it, you see him. Of course, you've mentally prepared yourself for this moment over the past two months while sweeping the floor, massaging your gums, and recovering from the drastic haircut you got the day after he left. But forget it. You know, in your heart of hearts, that he's a scoundrel, even if he does look like Gregory Peck and dance like Fred

Astaire (actually, in that case, I would put up with just about anything).

Listening to tales from the front, you begin to wonder how the world functions with so much dysfunction. Someone once told me, in all seriousness, "I love you, but I don't mind if you go out with other people. In fact, I sort of prefer it."

A friend of mine explained the chasm between men and women this way: Lots of men like the things that go *along* with intimacy, like Saturday night confessions, Sunday morning breakfasts, and shopping for Uncle Harold's eighty-ninth birthday. In order to obtain these things, they must *act* intimate: "I think we should talk about our feelings more often, keep the lines of communication open, explore the issues between us, don't you?" But it's not like they *mean* it. So my suggestion is, when you receive your next passion pink slip, leave the country. Which could be the greatest aphrodisiac of all. A calling card to men all over the world. There is nothing a man likes better than to date a woman who is on her way out of the city, state, or hemisphere. Suddenly you will have the allure of Michelle Pfeiffer, Julia Roberts, and Marilyn Monroe all rolled into one. Enjoy it before you go, since you know that is exactly what he is doing. However, if you knit him a sweater, suddenly you're Phyllis Diller. But if you're lucky, like I've been, the breakup happens right before the sweater is completed, and you'd rather wear a man's sweater three sizes too big than see it on a putz like him anyway. So, while you may be nursing a broken heart, at least it's warm, roomy, and well dressed.

THE SURE THING

Women who seek to be equal with men lack ambition.
——TIMOTHY LEARY

WHEN IT COMES TO ATTRACT-
ing men, logic escapes even the savviest of women. Probably because there is no logic involved, although one would think there should be, one of the greatest misconceptions of all time. There are no explanations for why the man you have cased out like an overzealous FBI agent, a man who fits the profile as the one person on this earth who would be your perfect complement, ends up marrying a woman he met three weeks before while traveling in the far reaches of Siberia. The minor problem that they don't speak the same language has made their star-crossed romance even more enticing. He confesses to you (since he has suddenly taken to you in a close-friend kind of way) and regularly pours out his heart to your skeptical ear. They don't know each other's languages yet, but think of all there is to explore! Think of the romance of it all, he says to you excitedly, to which all you can think in response is, Think of learning the pluperfect in your late thirties! When he toddles off to Siberia, ring in hand, you curse your own life for its lack of just that kind of sweeping excitement and try to reevaluate why a person as charming as this fellow wouldn't

fall at your feet immediately and offer to peel you grapes for all
of eternity. Then you hear through the grapevine that his Siber-
ian romance has taken a turn for the worse, that shortly after
the marriage it fizzled out completely and that your crush-person
is dejected and has decided to start a new life in Keokuk. You,
of course, proved to have been right in the first place, dance
under the moonlight and rejoice in your own superior wisdom,
secretly celebrating his misery, since it serves him right for not
recognizing that you are the Goddess of Love. Then, a year
later, when you hear that he has gained fifty pounds and
become an actuary, your really hit your stride, although by this
time you have started obsessing over someone else, someone
who also seems like exactly the kind of man who should be
wildly attracted to you, only to find that he has started up with a
conservative Republican senatorial office worker who wears red
suits with polyester blouses and nonmatching scarves wrapped
around her waist as though they were paisley beach cover-ups.
This is when you decide to throw in the towel and forget trying
to apply logic to affairs of the heart.

   You can read all the self-help books you want, you can run
on a treadmill till you've reduced your tuchas to bubkes, you
can stuff your face with oysters, and it won't make a bit of difference. For love, attraction, compatibility, and companionship
are not a science of objectivity; they are, rather, far and away
the single most subjective matter in the history of the universe.
Did Cavewoman X have a romp in the cave with Caveman Y
because of his universally sought-after ability to single-handedly
kill a wildebeest with his bare hands and bring it to the feet of
his intended? No, she probably just liked the way his mouth
turned up at the corners in concentration while he chiseled out
a piece of flint. The whole subject is just completely inexplica-

ble, no matter how many magazines scream to you that they hold the answers, in two pages nonetheless, as to what men REALLY want, what they REALLY think, and who they REALLY are (that, of course, is the hardest one of all).

Traditional methods have gotten us nowhere, as anyone who has had to fight on the front lines will tell you. Oh, sure, you can try and scour the earth for a guy worth his salt, which will surely make you more interested in spending the night at home, cleaning the neck of your ketchup bottle. Or you can rely on other people and go the route of blind dates, a fate I wouldn't wish on my worst editor (and that's bad). Modern blind dates are disasters waiting to happen. There is a very simple reason for this. In order for a blind-date setup to have any chance whatsoever, you have to be set up by someone who knows you well and knows him well and sees some potential connection between the two of you. This is the only way you can have more than a completely random chance of enjoying yourself. Otherwise you may as well just close your eyes and grab someone off the street. The problem is that anyone you know that well, well enough to trust them in setting you up on a date, is someone whose friends you have met as well. And if you have met all her friends, then chances are the person she set you up with is someone she doesn't know very well, a recipe for disaster.

Usually the blind date is set up by someone who sees a single characteristic in common and assumes that that is enough for a lifetime. Like, for instance, her thinking may go something like this: "Gwen is Jewish and single and so is my dentist's nephew's roommate's brother! Oh, but he is studying at the yeshiva this year. Hmmm. What about my ex-boss's dog walker's father-in-law's son from his first marriage? I think he is Jewish and single too—engrave the invitations!" I went on so many dates like this it is too embarrassing to detail. Why would I voluntarily go through such trauma? Because first of all, as I mentioned, being the open-minded person I am, I thought anything was worth a try once, and second, the advertisement was always presented as "a cute-but-not-in-a-traditional-way guy, really creative, funny, and interesting," not "nerdy geek with bad breath and slumped shoulders who is nonetheless completely full of himself because he once built a replica of Constantinople out of toothpicks and Life Savers." And when someone talks up a blind date to you, you can enjoy a rich fantasy life about who this person is, what he looks like, and how your time together will be spent—at least until you open the door, and within, say, thirty seconds or so, you know that you'd have more fun rodding out your drains.

But there is one more alternative open to the modern woman. A final solution to the age-old problem of finding a satisfying romance. One surefire method of drumming up business that I personally discovered and that I am fully prepared to share with you now. Brace yourself, because I am telling you, it is a miracle worker. An elixir that renders traditional dating obsolete. It's like a mental machete that cuts through the romantic jungle like a bulldozer, leaving nothing but rubble in its wake as you emerge victorious. It is the Dating Competition (not to be confused with the dating game). Let me explain.

The dating competition is simple in concept and beautiful in its smooth and easy application. It's the equivalent of a modern-day Stir and Frost. No mess, no complicated instructions, works every time.

Step #1.   Find a trusted and hilarious girlfriend and engage her in a dating competition.

Step #2.   Set up your own rules and regulations (suggested guidelines below).

Step #3.   Let the games begin, and

Step #4.   Watch the men fall where they may.

My friend Patrice and I did this with the best possible results. She ended up with a guy whom she went with for years, and I ended up dating a guy who seemed like a good egg for at least three or four months. Not bad!

And what is so successful about a such a plan? The simple, elegant fact that it turns women into menlike thinkers. I mean, in this game you are out for one thing, scoring. Naturally you and your fellow competitor should determine what constitutes a date and what constitutes a point, but here is the system Patrice and I used.

.25 point	a lunch date with a guy friend (at least it's something)
.5 point	a weekday lunch date with a potential boyfriend
.75 point	a date with someone you've known a long time but things seem to be taking a slightly romantic turn, even though at this stage it is all very ambiguous and unspoken
1 point	a weekday evening date
1.5 points	a weekend lunch date
2 points	a weekend evening date
2.5 points	and next-day-because-you-wanted-to-see-each-other-again-so-soon date
2.5 points	fling
3 points	the meeting-the-friends date
3.5 points	telling friends that your relationship with someone you've

known a long time has taken a turn for the romantic and you
are now so invested in it you are willing to go public

4 points   the meeting-the-family date

Nothing need be said about physical involvement, for even
the most competitive women would not sell herself short here
and exchange an unwanted experience just to gloat the next
day over the points that she's now earned (as some boys have
been known to do).

And in the act of seeking out your victory, you will automatically mentally position yourself in an excellent spot for
attracting men: not giving a shit about them. They serve
merely as your own personal conduit to victory. You will find
yourself becoming much more aggressive about asking guys
out, seeking out new guys, and going places you wouldn't normally go, all the while maintaining the cool detachment that
drives men crazy with lust. At this point you can sit back and
watch your social calendar fill up like the *Titanic*.

The men will sniff you out like bloodhounds. They will
catch a whiff of your indifference and start clawing at the
ground in frustration when they find you can't get together
until three weeks from Thursday. They will start pounding
down your door, lining up around the block, enticing you with
pricey gifts. You can have your way with any one of them,
whatever your way happens to be. They will go home confused as to how better to impress you. They will rack their
brains thinking of ploys to win you over. They will call their
friends to tell them about the woman they met who seems
completely cavalier and how her virtual detachedness has
turned their knees into jelly and their heart into mush. And
all the while you will be yawning at the sameness of it all as

you interview men over the phone while regrouting your bathroom tiles, racking up points by the dozen, calling your friend daily to flaunt your steadily rising numbers.

And this may very well change your life. For as you become a beacon of indifference, the poster child for the cavalier, you may just stumble upon one guy, standing in the back of the pack, waiting for all the idiots to kill one another or swim the wrong way like wayward sperm while he plans his strategy carefully, waits for the right moment, and emerges as a man worth taking a second look at, despite your pledge of nonchalance. He is smart enough to know that by standing at the back of the pack and acting indifferently himself, he is sure to catch your eye, which has been his plan all along.

It could take a week, a month, even a year or two, but this is by far the best method I have yet come across. And if you are still unconvinced, not only will I throw in a set of Ginsu knives and a radish roser, I need only remind you what is going through the mind of your neighbor's doctor's son's college roommate right about now . . .

FRIENDS' ENDS

If you can't be a good example, then
you'll just have to be a horrible warning.
—CATHERINE AIRD

ONE MUST BE A TRIFLE careful that one doesn't cross a few unspoken boundaries in search of victory. One should stay away from anyone who could put her behind bars, for instance. And one should stay away from good friends. Not just because it wreaks havoc on your relationship, which will never again be the same, but good friends, as anyone who has tried to seduce one knows, make for bad lovers. This is no indication of your best friends' *abilities* as lovers—I mean, for all I know, once you cross that invisible, fine line, you could have a real barn burner and never be able to forget it as long as you live (good luck). In fact, your best friend probably is a prince among men, the exception to every rule, the needle in the haystack. He undoubtedly has a great sense of humor. He is surely smart and kind and generous and sympathetic. He may know how to cook *and* dress. He may even have great hair and beautiful hands. He may, in short, fulfill all your essential requirements in a (finally) decent date, which will all of a sudden one day—inevitably—make you sit bolt upright in the middle of the night, as if someone dropped an anvil on your head, and blurt out, "Wait a minute! What about *him*?! Of course! What an idiot I've been. He's the one . . ." You will rub your eyes and shake the sleep out of your head as though just coming to from a long and harrowing coma, not unlike Sleeping Beauty, and say to yourself, "Why, how could I have been so dumb? All these years I have been searching, searching, searching while my fate, my destiny, my Prince Charming was right here all the time, but I have been too blind to see! I was lost but now am found! Dorothy was right—'If you can't find it in your own backyard, then it isn't worth having in the first place.' I gotta go tell Harold that I am the ONE for him!" and off you run into the land of embarrassment, humiliation, and quite possibly complete and total ruin.

But don't let me stop you.

I'd like to, of course, and save you a few years of deep depression, but the sad fact is that it is hardwired into our very chromosomes that we think we *will* be the .001 percent for whom things like this actually work out. We will be the one to tame the wild beast, to make a smooth transition from friends to lovers, to meet David Cassidy and have him be our love slave for life.

And we are blindly confident of not just our survival in matters of this kind, but our inevitable success where millions have failed before us. There is a place in Alberta, Canada, called Head-Smashed-In Buffalo-Jump. I find it pretty self-explanatory. At one time, unwitting buffalo were run off a cliff where they fell to their deaths, smashing their heads in. I came upon this spot unknowingly and have never forgotten about it. How could I? To me, this is the animal kingdom's equivalent of trying to seduce one of your good friends. You might as well just take a running leap off the cliff and hope for the best.

I should know. My head has been smashed in many times.

But not without good reason. And if you are ultimately going to get that pretty little head of yours smashed in, you ought to have a good reason at the very least. And this is why, if you haven't ever engaged in this kind of misguided behavior, I am going to save you from years of misery, even though you are still going to think that you are the one person for whom all these rules don't apply. Well, don't say I didn't warn you.

This is why the seduction of good friends is so very seductive in and of itself: Everyone wants her lover to be her best friend. Someone with whom you can talk about anything, someone who is supportive, understands your neuroses and loves you anyway, someone who is not judgmental of you, someone who shares your interests, and someone for whom you have an unusual tolerance for being around all the time. This job description is easily filled by a good friend of the opposite sex. He fulfills every requirement, if he is indeed a really good friend. And then you realize that the only thing missing to make this picture complete is a little nookie. So you figure, quite logically, that if you seduce this man, then you have a genuine, bona fide, surefire hit on your hands, one that will take you out of the dismal "continually looking" subset of human beings and into the I-found-gold-at-the-end-of-the-rainbow set. The group we love to hate but secretly want to be a part of.

The problem with such rock-hard logic is that there is nothing logical about romance. And it doesn't take long to figure out that the introduction of nookie into a once serene, platonic relationship is the equivalent of a romantic hand grenade. There are two reasons for this. One is that matters of the heart reside in such a strange place within the human psyche that it acts as a virtual dumping ground for even the the most well-balanced, controlled, logical, thoughtful, confident person's every weirdness. In every other aspect of their lives, people like this are the epitome of normalcy. They may be quite accomplished, quite talented, quite resourceful, independent, and beyond moral reproach. They could be well-loved public figures, community leaders, religious figureheads, movie stars, scholars, or just your next-door neighbors—but when it comes to relationships, the most upright of these people display inexplicable insecurities, foibles, neuroses, psychoses, masochism, sadism, instability, callousness, depravity . . . the list goes on and on. This is where all their demons come out and spread their destructive wings, as if all their lives they have been pent up and suddenly they get to run free and wreak havoc on the emotional life of the innocent bystander. There is no predicting, no telling, no guessing as to how people's behavior will change once they become romantically involved with one another.

And there are some things you just don't want to find out about someone you really like. Particularly a good friend. Who wants to know the level of depravity that her best friend is truly capable of? Do you really want to find out that he is so tormented underneath it all that the only relief he can find is if you flog him with leather cheerleading pom-poms while singing Brahms's Lullaby? No, some things are best left as mysteries. Once you find out, of course, that the guy you have confided in for many years, whom you have admired and sought solace in, is suddenly treating you like a leper when you let it slip that you have had a ten-year urge to rip his clothes off, you can never go back to your past opinion of him. It's gone. And the person that you usually come to to grouse about every hangnail has suddenly become the hangnail himself, for which it is totally inappropriate to speak to the man. It's like seeing your favorite radio personality in person. You are much better off fantasizing about how great he looks, what a wonderful person he is, and how scintillating it would be to have dinner with him than actually meeting him, being disappointed that he is not a five-foot-ten blond with a flat stomach and a penchant for sleeping with his admirers, and getting brushed off rudely besides.

And, in my opinion, there is some natural law of physics out there that explains all this. There is a reason why you and the man in question are good friends and nothing more. And the cosmos knows it; he most likely knows it; you are the only slow one on the block. It is like there is a natural force keeping you from jumping in the sack together. Because if it was supposed to happen, it would have happened by now, and the fact that it hasn't is a testimonial that there is some natural, organic reason why it probably shouldn't. Maybe you are too much alike, maybe the banter that fuels your flirtatious friendship would sink a romance because after the first three glorious times you went to bed laughing hysterically and thinking that you had just hit pay dirt, you would find that there were big awkward silences that lasted maybe a week or two once you tried to actually discuss something serious (it has to happen sometime), or maybe you just got a really close look at his toenails and it freaked you right out. The only problem is that there are plenty of us who each feel that we alone have the power to beat such a force of nature. However, even though a man may know, in his heart of hearts, that he adores you as a friend and nothing more, that you remind him a little too much of his aunt Thelma, the one with the big arms, to sleep with you, that you aren't his type, or that you are too close to him to actually get close to him (that is always a good one), I have never known a man to turn away even his best friend if she has a hankering for peeling his clothes off with her teeth. Never. Reject a woman who (even temporarily) has just found religion and thinks he is GOD? No way. This is too much to expect out of a man. Really.

And so, the saga goes like this. You wake up one day and realize that if only your good friendship were to successfully turn romantic, your life would be perfect. You begin to obsess about a man you may have known half your life. Then you plan how best to introduce the idea to him so as not to scare him off. Do you use the adult, intellectual approach and actually try to talk about it? Or do you just take a ballsy chance and get a little too close to him, brush against him, supposedly by accident, and then offer up a back rub that ever so subtly turns into a front rub? Once nookie has been introduced, you may realize right away or it may take a little while, but before too long, it becomes clear that this was not meant to be. It could be the moment when you find him howling at the moon in the middle of the night, or it could be the moment when he confesses that when he is alone, he likes to eat his own hair. Perhaps it is just an exchange of glances between the two of you after a strained tryst when you seem to be saying to each other, "I sure adore you, but something isn't right here, because after a lifetime of talking to you about everything in my life, I am tongue-tied to come up with the most menial of trivialities to break this awkward silence that has settled over our every encounter." Then you have no choice but to walk around the city with him, enduring torturous examinations of both your feelings while one of you has to confess that the other person just doesn't fit into that category of people whose clothes you want to rip off while the other one tries desperately to sink into the sidewalk, never to be heard from again. Then, after a few weeks (or years) of this, you finally make the break from this person for your own mental health and go about repairing the gaping hole in your life that he has left. This is usually the way it goes, in some version or another.

The first time I tried to seduce one of my best friends, it ended in a disastrous split that left me living at home with my parents and spending my Saturday nights praying they would go out so I would be left alone to enjoy a case of Nutty Buddies and *Fantasy Island*. For years I had had a crush on this guy; we'll call him the Beaver. Through high school and college I got to know him better and better as I spoon-fed him each and every one of my close friends, whom he happily lusted after. We grew very close. Not close enough for my taste, but close nonetheless. Of course, as we have already determined, I was flattered to be thought of as the good friend while the real girlfriends came and went, despite the fact that we were both treating me like a sexless lump of flesh. My philosophy, demented though it was (so very young was I), was that when I got my shit together, lost a little weight, and figured some things out, then he would see the blinding light of my iridescent beauty and devastating allure and we would be together forever, one of the few happy couples in an otherwise miserable world. (This is a trap that American women fall into about eighteen times a day: When I lose weight, he will love me, that's right! It's just those darn twelve pounds that stand between us. And then, with a monumental letdown, one day we lose the weight and we realize that the weight has nothing to do with anything and, like America without the Soviet Union, we are at a loss for a mental enemy.) Because we got along so well, it seemed to me that romance was the next logical extension of such a close friendship. In my own defense I have to say here that the Beaver was sending me plenty of signals as well that read, You Are the Most Special Person in My Life, Just Not the One I'm Sleeping With. But he did not share my enthusiasm for such a logical extension of such a close friendship.

Not knowing this, I mustered all the bravery I could, secured my heart in my hand, and took the Greyhound bus to his school (formerly my school until I dropped out in confusion), where I presented it to him on a silver platter. Not immediately, mind you. No, first there was lots of talking, being introduced to his new roommates (like I cared a hoot in hell about them), a loving late-night snowball fight in the street, a few too many beers on his part (avoidance ring a bell to you?), and finally retiring for the evening. We both knew what was going on, though as you might predict, it didn't really come up in conversation.

There was no one thing that happened that could qualify as a watershed event, no real turning point that makes much sense, just "before that night" and "after that night." After the snowball fight and the beers, we went to bed (the same bed) and woke up estranged. At least I did. And it's not even like there was a lot of hanky-panky, either. It's just that nothing about it seemed right. It wasn't the slow and dreamy romance I had expected and fantasized about, it was an attempt at a roll in the hay with a drunk guy who was snoring before my camisole came off (and I wore a camisole, mind you!). Suddenly, the Beaver was like an alien. He'd been my buddy, my confidant, the host to a whole set of transferred affections, and now he was like a cyclops from Mars. I lay wide awake in his bed until, at 5:00 A.M. I went downstairs and stared out the window at the snow, pretending I was in a movie with subtitles. Then I made small talk with his roommates until he woke up toward noon and we could take a long walk, where he could say things to the effect of "We-are-so-symbiotic-that-I-literally-don't-know-if-I-could-live-without-you-but-now-that-I've-seen-you-naked-it-turns-out-I-can." And my personal favorite, as we were getting kicked out of a restaurant at closing time, "We always have the most personal of conversations in the most public of places."

It was December and I went home with my tail between my legs, as dazed and confused as ever, wondering why I felt like an emotional piñata. Then, while I was trying to piece my brain back together, he showed me that he was quickly back on his feet by seducing my last remaining best friend when they were both home for winter break. A minor setback. Nothing ten years of distance and my college tuition's worth of therapy didn't clear right up. A smart girl may have learned at this point that trying to change the laws of nature can have its drawbacks. *Pas moi.*

I went on to embarrass myself in numerous other relationships. These would be the relationships where you meet someone, hit it off pretty well, start doing things together, but three or four dates go by and nothing has happened. Nothing more than a quick kiss or hug good night.

Lots of getting a little too close to him on your part, maybe, but no general mutual action. Life is full of these mysterious evenings. You go to movies, plays, new restaurants; take walks; go for bike rides; shop for holiday gifts; and generally pour a lot of energy into these outings. But when nothing starts to bloom, a girl starts wondering why. Is it because he doesn't like her? A possibility she quickly passes off because she knows she is eminently likable and says to herself, of course he likes me, otherwise why would he be spending all this time with me and pouring all this energy my way? Could it be that he is just a slow starter, which indicates that he is either a real mensch, the kind you would want to spend the rest of your life with, which only fuels the flames of your interest further, or has deep-seated conflicts with the expression of any feelings, which you of course think that you can unearth? Or perhaps he is seeing someone else and has not mentioned it because things with her are rocky and he is trying to decide between the two of you. Or, then again, maybe underneath it all he is one of the idiots who has not figured out yet that this situation requires direct confrontation or will lead to a mass of confused feelings and dashed expectations, since he thinks you are just the *greatest,* since you are so much fun, so smart, such good company, so funny, so interesting and so diverse and refreshing, but not in a romantic kind of way, since probably he is more romantically attracted to people with the charisma of oatmeal. After a few hundred of these that ended badly, a girl like me can only take this kind of suspense for so long in new situations. After that, I have to know.

This usually leads to a very awkward evening whereupon you say something like "So, is there something going on between you and me or do you look at this as just a good-friends type of thing? 'Cause you know, I'm better in bed than I look, and you would be remiss to let this opportunity go by without seeing for yourself," and then your work is over and you can just sit back and watch him flail around, taken aback by your surprise attack. It is especially interesting when you are with a man who has genuinely never thought about these things. This guy will stammer and blush and it will test his proclivity for extemporaneous speech to the utmost.

There was one occasion when, after listening to friend after friend say to me, "You and Bobo would make such a great couple, you are like peas in a pod. How come you never went out?" I woke up one day near my thirtieth birthday with not a romantic possibility in sight and decided that they were all right and that it was time to do something about it, goddammit. After all, we were sort of perfect for each other, except that he always went out with blonde coatracks. Once again, I tried my best, but to no avail. He flirted with me and I with him, but the blonde coatracks won out, and it was all probably for the best since the last time I talked to him he showed no signs of ever being interested in doing anything as limiting as getting married or having children (part of me can't blame him, of course, but that's another story). And that is the lesson to be learned from these best friends/would-be lovers. If the right ingredients were there in the first place, you would have had a romance long ago.

Like me, you are probably stubborn and determined. However, before you ruin your life, take a good hard look at yourself and what you are about to do and listen to me for a change. Don't do it. Sit on your hands, gag yourself, lock yourself in your apartment, and rip out the phone. And if all that fails, you can always commit yourself. Just don't make any handsome, well-forearmed good men friends while you are in the clink. And if you do, present yourself as a new person, a tempting seductress for whom the Kama Sutra was like a kindergarten primer. Let him know right off the bat that if he doesn't bathe you in rose petals and worship you like the erotic goddess you are, you will walk all over him in your stilettos on your way to the next sultry conquest that awaits you (this may in and of itself excite him). And if he delays for but one moment, hems and haws with one sentence that begins "I find you really attractive, but . . ." then up you walk and out you go.

And trust me, while you may have to act as though you are Sharon Stone the first time around, following a script and playing a part that feels completely unnatural to you, you will soon be so liberated by your newfound control and power that you will develop a blow-off style all your own. It will go down in the Blow-Off Hall of Fame, where you will have a whole wing named after you. And then one day, a few men later, when Sharon Stone walks up to you and bows at your feet and begs for some private tutoring, don't be surprised. Be your gracious self and say, "Sharon, my friend, it's all about the laws of nature. You're a girl who has a lot going for her. Just listen to me . . ."

DO WE HAVE TO STOP NOW?

Today, if you're not confused, you're not thinking clearly.
——IRENE NORRIS

PLAYING THE SEDUCTRESS
is an important skill to have under one's belt, if you catch my drift. And if your id is not cooperating with you for any reason, if your ego has taken a battering lately at the hands of Beavers and Tweedledees, then it is time for a little mental makeover. Snip, snip here, clip, clip there and a couple of tra-la-las. Time to take yourself in to see whether the problem can be fixed with a tune-up or if you need an outright overhaul. Forget Marge (You're soaking in it!) the manicurist, forget Mister (Let me look under your hood) Goodwrench, I'm talking therapy.

A good therapist is like a warm bath. You slip in, feel better, and come out either refreshed and ready to take the world on or in search of a bed where you can sleep for the next twenty years or so. This is one of the strangest aspects of the therapy process: It can leave you so elated that you virtually float through the rest of the day or so depressed you take off your own belt and shoelaces.

I love therapy. *Love* it. Would do it every week for the rest of my life if I had the time and the money. There is nothing better. A full hour of self-indulgence with someone who is paid to be attentive. What could be more satisfying? Girl-friends, you might say. But even I have to admit that the problem with girlfriends is that they are too loyal. They usually don't want to have to point out that your low self-esteem, combined with a certain superiority complex, has given you a narcissistic character disorder with a strong depressive tendency that you have had since your freshman year in high school. That is the beauty of a girlfriend. She will just say, "Don't I know it," and offer you half of her Milky Way. And this is not only because you tend to hang out with fellow narcissistic-character-disordered women with strong depressive tendencies that they've had since high school; no, this is just the way girlfriends are. They are the right people to chew the fat, not lose the weight. Enter the therapist.

The one part of therapy I don't like: stopping. For every therapist has cultivated the most polite and benign way he or she can think of to bring a session to a close, sentences like "We have to stop now." And while it is a nice way of indicating that your fifty minutes are up, it is also, I'm sure, in some cases, their polite way of saying, "I'm sick and tired of listening to you whine about the same problems I've heard for the past eight years. You're outta time, so why don't you just pay me and get outta here . . . and for God's sake, pick up those snot rags as you go." And frankly, who can blame them? It's a tough business they're in. How would you like to have to sit there and listen to someone harp on the same damn self-centered problems year in and year out? Of course, for $120 an hour, I might be persuaded. Nevertheless, I think that the only tougher thing than being a therapist is being the thera-pee. The toughest job you'll ever love. Looking at it historically,

I don't know who the first therapist was, maybe Eve when Adam started griping about his missing rib and what it meant to his manhood. Women tend to be good listeners, which is why I have always seen woman therapists. If you want succor, see a woman. If you want analysis, see a man. Plus, a woman has been a woman all her life, and I think one thing we can be relatively sure of is that a man hasn't. This is reason enough for me. And with a woman, you don't have to run the risk of falling for your therapist, which you do anyway in some form or another, so why complicate things? I like to think of myself as a TV that is on the fritz and just needs a good whack in the head before getting back into focus. Therapists are good at whacking. And you will take their whacks over your mother's or your girlfriends' because that's what you are paying them to do. That is their job. It may seem a little like paying someone to give you a mental root canal, but you know, an abscess is worse. (Too many people are walking around with suppurating mental sores, in my opinion. The kind who usually say things like, "I don't need to see a therapist, I just talk to you and I always feel better." A sure sign that something infectious is brewing.) And hopefully, in the end, you walk away with a gigantic set of emotional tools, which is precisely why I would love to be in therapy my whole life. I'd never have to rely on myself again, and what a relief *that* would be.

Men, I've noticed, don't often share this attitude about psychological intervention. They like to think of themselves as completely self-reliant. They think about therapy the way they think about homosexuality. They *want* to be open-minded, but there is something in them that is completely resistant. Their basic philosophy is "It's fine for you, it's just not something

I'm interested in, that's all. It's not for me." In other words, gay guys are just fine, but if one touches me, I'll kill 'im. I can't even begin to tell you how many times I, the well adjusted, have delicately suggested to various friends and boyfriends over the years that they go see a therapist about any one of a number of deeply rooted insecurities that make them act like an odd combination of Bruce Willis and Tiny Tim, only to hear that exact response. So, a man's significant other usually ends up going without him to discuss the source of the problem (him), and since he isn't there, there is only so much work that can be done.

There is, I have to admit, a fine line. Because the other extreme is equally intolerable, and that is the man who has "discovered" therapy and, like a zealous convert, won't shut up about it and has to dissect every situation down to its most fundamental therapeutic elements. This is completely insufferable. At first, a girl can be sucked in to this man's seeming sensitivity, for who else would stay up with her discussing repressed feelings she has from twelve years ago? My God, she thinks to herself, not only is this a man who doesn't mind my talking about repressed feelings from twelve years ago, he has repressed feelings too, *and* he is actually aware of them! Could it be that he also offered me an insight that I hadn't thought of, introduced a new thought into my head? Surely not! But when she sees that this is so, she is putty in his hands. She thinks she has died and gone to heaven. She immediately thinks this is the One, until she realizes that he can't stop at a stoplight without bringing up the Jungian interpretation of it all and is about as much fun as a chewed-up corn cob. She suddenly gets wise to the fact that he is a therapy obsessive and knows she has to find a way to dump him in a polite manner so as not to add to the years that he will be going to his therapist.

I have been to quite a few therapists in my lifetime, and to me, a good therapist is almost better than a good hairdresser. I have known women to fly across two and three states just to go to their preferred hairdresser, and who can blame them? Anyone who has walked out of a beauty salon looking like Don King understands. A good hairdresser is vital, and so is a good therapist, since ultimately they do much the same thing. Massage your head and trim off the frayed, split ends. Oftentimes you get a new look and you walk out feeling a little more put together than you did an hour ago. Some think of the hairdresser *as* a therapist, and if you're really lucky, your therapist may throw in an occasional bang trim as well. Like a good hairdresser, a good therapist is someone you should feel loyal to and be willing to follow to the ends of the earth. In my experience, it always helps to feel an immediate and very strong connection with this person so that you don't look up from a heart-wrenching monologue about the single most traumatic event of your childhood only to see him balancing his checkbook, which would be unfortunate. No, you have to like this person enough not to feel conspicuous when you take up the whole hour talking about a hangnail.

This can be trying on days when you feel like you've run out of things to say and you find yourself going on about which moisturizer is better for dry skin just to avoid the dreaded therapy silence. This is not like a silence in any other conversation. Not in any way. A silence in a normal conversation can be awkward, yes. But there are many gimmicks one can resort to if one is resourceful. Get up and look out the window pensively as though you are thinking about whether or not to divulge the secret recipe to Coca-Cola which you happen to know by heart; say that you are parched and need something to drink, offering insincerely to get your conversation mate something as well; or, if all else fails, feign illness. In the therapist's office you have to have a stomach of granite to withstand any more than about three seconds of silence. After that, any self-respecting neurotic begins to feel totally paranoid that this silence will be interpreted as a hostile act, or maybe a sign of a passive-aggressive tendency. It is best to keep the flow of conversation up so as not to add three more years to your sentence.

But one day, as you walk out the door, the sun will shine and the birds will sing and you will say to yourself, I no longer feel the need to pay for my therapist's new chateau in Provence! And then you just have one more year to go while you negotiate your exit. Just make sure that when you do make your final exit, the door behind you is unlocked so that you can always get back in.

OF CARPENTERS AND MEN

If they can put a man on the moon,
why can't they put one in me?
— FLASH ROSENBERG

IN YOUR QUEST FOR UNIVER-
sal truths, be it via a therapist, a spiritual advisor, or a sooth-sayer, you may come to discover the path to enlightenment, the secret to inner peace, the ties that bind all men. Forget about all that. I am here to tell you about something much more interesting, a truth so profound as to be biblical, the tie that binds all women, all across the universe. And I think you know what I am talking about. A special breed of man: Carpenters. Oh, sister.

Every woman worth her salt has a thing about carpenters. All kinds of women, any kind of carpenter. It is like an unspoken, universal attraction. A woman talking of a new love interest need only to finish her description with "... *and,* he's a *carpenter,*" and all women within earshot will stop what they're doing, gather around, and collectively drool, insisting on minute physical details so that they can enjoy an active fantasy life some time later that evening. Simply put, carpenters are the embodiment of sexiness. Chiseled bodies, sculpted muscles, forearms that could reduce a girl to tears, and hands like

Hercules. Plus, they really *do* know their way around a toolbox. That alone can leave a girl begging for more. Who knew a monkey wrench could be so provocative? But it is. Oh, it is.

There is something about a man and his tools that strips away all of your more cerebral ideas about the perfect man and gets right to the gut of what the cavewoman in you cries out for: Rawness. Strength. Simplicity. This man may not be able to take care of your emotional needs, but he can build you a desk with just the right number of drawers and slots, which is often just as good. Carpenters, if they are smart, know that they can have their pick of the litter. And if they happen to casually mention the fact that they did their senior thesis on Nietzsche or Kierkegaard, well, just sit back and watch the bodies fall.

So when I was introduced to a bright, stocky, newly single carpenter named Peter at a friend's dinner party, it was practically a force beyond my control that made me call him a few days later and ask him out. It was like being a sleepwalker. Dial phone, make small talk, ask out. Happily, he was receptive. Peter was a very nice guy with hands the size of hams, thinning brown hair, and rimless glasses that gave him that look of intelligence. We went to see a play and then to dinner, where we discussed the show, our families, and his voracious reading habits. Okay, fine, where do you want me? I found him fascinating and dreamed of built-in bookshelves. My friends thought he was dreamy. These two things were enough to go on for quite a while. Throw in the fact that he enjoyed cooking *and* he loved to dance (believe it or not, he was very good at it. This quality in and of itself has led me to date men for months and even years longer than I knew was good for me. But who can feel good about leaving a man who can really rock? As any woman knows, a nongay male who can dance well is so rare that once you find one, psychosis of all kinds take a backseat to such a standout talent) and no female would stand a chance. I was toast.

Things went well for a while, and of course all my girl-friends displayed a keener than usual interest in my love life, presumably to see if life with a carpenter lived up to its promise. Which it did, particularly in the first week or two. It was exciting. Like winning a Nobel or a Pulitzer, or maybe a MacArthur Genius Grant, or toting an Oscar around town. Meet someone new, mention your new boyfriend, tell her he's a *carpenter*, and watch the blood just drain from her face. Oh, the petty satisfaction.

We were having a fine time, talked about books a lot, cooked, danced, and rode our bikes at sunrise to see the cherry blossoms in full bloom before the tourists arrived. But naturally things started going awry after a while.

The beginning of the end was when he confessed over the phone that he really didn't like to kiss. True, his skill in the kissing department had fallen far short of the expectations his forearms promised. (I mean, anyone with forearms like that should be a good kisser, or else why bother?) We'd kissed many times and he did seem kind of squirmy. Didn't like to kiss? Now that he was actually saying the words "I don't like kissing," it was just plain sacrilege. He was a heretic. It was a flashing red light screaming out his lack of finesse and sensuality if ever there was one.

Now, kissing styles can differ—often do, in fact, and differ-ent kissing styles need to be tweaked and massaged into fitting together perfectly. This is not so unusual, especially with boys, who have all the subtlety of maybe a jackhammer. I could understand this. But no, he insisted that wasn't it. Then I thought maybe he just didn't like kissing *me,* but I dismissed that immediately as ludicrous. Kissing is not a pastime, it's an art form. When done right. Every kiss has a little life of its own with a beginning, middle, and end, and the best kiss should leave you in a heap on the floor. Even if it's just a short one. For him not to like it revealed far more about him than I cared to see. But, kissing aversion notwithstanding, he was a *carpenter,* and that alone automatically bought him another chance.

Then one day we got together with friends and one of mine confessed that with the impending birth of his first child, he had gone into therapy to settle long-unresolved feelings he had about his own father. This spun into some general conversation about father–son relationships. The carpenter started talking about how he thought that all this recent talk about child abuse was completely overdone—after all, his father had beat the crap out of *him* and *he* wouldn't have called it child abuse. My girlfriend and I exchanged skeptical glances. Our minds were in total sync. They were both flashing one word to each other. THERAPY! THERAPY! THERAPY! When he continued later on talking about the trampled rights of accused rapists, insisting that the number of actual rapes is nowhere near the number of accusations brought by women against men, I knew the end was close at hand. But I didn't expect him to dump me before I could dump him. Soon thereafter I got the boot in the middle of the night, when, just after having yet another unsatisfying roll in the hay, he told me that he thought we should just be friends because he didn't think he could give me what I was looking for. If I didn't even know what the hell I was looking for, how did he? Needless to say, when he told me that, I immediately got out of bed and started to dress.

"You don't have to go!" he said. "I didn't mean that you should go."

"Oh? You are too kind."

"Let me at least walk you home, it's two A.M.!"

"And they say chivalry is dead. What are they thinking?"

"Oh, here we go . . ."

Now men, take note. No matter how much you may loathe the person you are sleeping with, no matter how dead the relationship has become, this is not a good time to break up with a girl. In fact, this is a bad time. A time that will instantly put you at the top of her shit list for years to come, and there is nothing you can do to get back in her good graces, to say nothing of her pants. Yet if you took a poll and asked women what percentage of their boyfriends had dumped them in just such a manner (or maybe at the wedding of a friend, a big surprise party you threw for him, a major family holiday like Christmas or Thanksgiving, after you just moved in with him, that kind of thing), I would venture to guess that the answer would be between 40 and 50 percent. There is a perfect explanation for this: We all know that big occasions bring out big feelings and big feelings often mean saying sayonara. However, my carpenter's approach is a perfect illustration of how some men have to somehow feel close to you before they lower the boom. I would like to break up with you, but I have to feel in sync with you enough to have this difficult and heart-wrenching discussion, so let's hop in the sack. *Twisted* is the only word that comes to mind.

And so, as I was walking home at 2 A.M. on a mild summer evening, I devised a plan: Flee. Why not? I was young,

had no attachments, no mortgage, no children, but I had a little nest egg that I was saving for all those things that I kindly
enough gave myself permission to blow on a frivolous vacation. The next day I set the wheels in motion. First, I thought
of everyone I knew all over Europe that I could mooch off of.
Then I convinced some girlfriends that this was the opportunity of a lifetime and that they absolutely *had* to come with me
on this last fling or they would regret it all their lives. Three of
them fell for it, at least as far as Paris. I had a ticket from D.C.
to Paris and, three months later, from Israel to D.C. Between
Paris and Israel, I had no plans. All in all, in three months I
spent $90 on lodging, a fact I am still proud of. Moocher
extraordinaire.

I decided to end my trip in Israel because my good friend
Lori had recently moved there, spoke fluent Hebrew, had a
car, was unemployed, and had nothing better to do than to
show me around and play with me for three weeks. (I met
Lori at the first and last Jewish singles event I ever went to, a
weekend bike ride on a scenic part of the Eastern Shore. I
figured, if you have to spend the whole weekend with people
of the same religion as you, you should choose something athletic, an automatic guarantee that while they might be studying the Talmud, at the very least they have the balance and
coordination required to ride a bike . . . right? Lori ran this
trip and still ranks as one of the strongest women I know. She
could ride circles around us all. Plus, she saved me from
rooming with a woman who was not a bike rider, had no
enthusiasm or athletic ability, and, in fact, may actually have
been dead. We have been friends ever since.) I'd never really
had any interest in going to Israel, since everyone I knew was
always encouraging me to do so. Nothing makes me turn the

other way more than well-meaning people telling me I should
do something. Drives me crazy. Plus, in early high school,
people I knew had gone to Israel and had life-changing experiences, and there again, I hated the thought of anything that
would change someone into the kind of person who would
harp on me to please go through the exact same change they
went through. No, thank you. Having said that, I had the time
of my life.

Every day was a bigger adventure than the day before. Of
course, one of the very first stops for a tourist in Israel is the
Wailing Wall. Dressed appropriately for the dry, warm weather
and the coming Sabbath, Lori and I set off in light flowery
dresses (there is something about a light flowery dress that can
really do the trick sometimes) and headed toward the old city.
But before we left to go, Lori insisted that we write down a
wish (some say prayer) to put in the cracks between the stones.
This is repeated thousands of times a day by Jews from around
the world. (In fact, now you can fax your prayers from anywhere and a little runner will take them to the wall and stick
them between two stones; welcome to the global interface.) So
the wall is pretty darn crowded with tiny pieces of paper,
maybe half the size of a gum wrapper and smaller. I was temporarily stifled. Of what magnitude does a wish need to be
when it goes directly to God? Should it be of the "I wish for
world peace" variety or more like "Could you please see your
way clear to trimming three inches off my upper arms?" The
first seemed unlikely, particularly in the middle of the Middle
East, and the second seemed too frivolous even for me
(although it would be nice). So I racked my brain to think of
something that would be important enough that God might
pick it out of the millions of requests and pay attention to it,

but something realistic and not too selfish-seeming that would fit in a very small space. This is what I came up with:

Please find me a nice, *normal* guy.
You know where I live.

I picked my spot on the wall and jammed the little wad of paper in, trying to be respectful of the people who were praying real prayers. This was as good a method as any, I figured. Years before, a friend of mine's very Catholic aunt had sent me a little figurine of Saint Anthony, the patron saint of things lost, along with the ditty, *Something lost, something found, please Saint Anthony, help me look around.* The idea here was that I needed to find the man who was made for me and Saint Anthony was just the guy to help. Unfortunately, he had been at it maybe six years and hadn't come up with squat. I could have warned him, "Listen, Saint A., men are dogs, so why don't you just throw in the towel now and take yourself a breather?" But you know, everyone has to find these things out for themselves. So I figured, I'll give God himself a try. Why not? Saint Anthony had his chance, time to bring in a pinch hitter.

I didn't think much more about the Wailing Wall message until I got home and found a message on my answering machine from a man previously unknown to me. I was suspicious. I was even more suspicious when I found out that he was a friend of a friend of my family's. If that isn't the kiss of death, I don't know what is. I pictured a man in a black hat and ringlet sideburns. Yet I didn't want to be rude, and after all, it *was* a man and he *was* calling me. Plus, an unseen voice on an answering machine is worth at least a few days of fantasizing as you play it over and over again for your girlfriends and try to fill in the details from the sound of his voice as if it's a secret code. Actually, the modern-day answering machine is like an updated version of *The Dating Game*. Nothing to go on but the sound of his voice. Fortunately for us, Herb Alpert and over-sized Peter Max–like daisies were not a part of it. This was, granted, a pathetic source of entertainment, but it was better than *thirtysomething* reruns, at least. Eventually, despite the family connection, I called him back.

Turns out, we grew up in the same neighborhood. This was a little hard to swallow. Someone in my neighborhood that I didn't even know? Impossible. Perhaps I forgot to tell you that I was queen of the neighborhood in which I grew up and knew all my subjects by name. I quizzed him in detail about the little-known facts of the South Side of Chicago. Mitchell's Ice Cream Parlor? Cunis's? Shoreland Delicatessen? The Chelton? Henry N. Hart? The real Markons on Pill Hill? He knew them all.

Then he told me who he'd gone to school with, many of whom were childhood friends of mine (I immediately dismissed him as having been in school way too long and ventured an educated guess that he would not have enough street smarts for me). The similarities were uncanny. We seemed to have led quite parallel lives but just missed each other at every turn. And as it turns out, that was a good thing. We later agreed that in those earlier days, I would surely have dismissed him right away as too nerdy and he would have dismissed me as too Jewish. I guess he was into dating blond-haired blue-eyed Girls Without Girlfriends of German descent.

Then we discovered the common denominator that would forever cast our relationship in a different and not always pleasant light, something not to be taken lightly when considering someone for a romp in the hay. Our parents actually *knew* each other, and had known each other for more than forty years. Let me repeat, *forty years.*

"Oh, you remember them, Gwen, they're friends of the Garbers and the Brodkeys," my mother said, trying to sound nonchalant as her salivary glands started audibly pumping. "They lived in Marynook. Still do, in fact. They're really very nice. I think he's a few years older than you. Why, did he call you?" Ha! As transparent as cellophane. I could picture the dark, musty room that they gathered in, the four of them, to finalize the deal.

"Well, you know she *was* Bat Mitvahed," my mother would boast.

"And he was *Bar* Mitzvahed," his father would counter. "Plus, he has a Ph.D., from Stanford, no less."

"I hope he isn't an egghead," my mother would mutter under her breath. "Of course, she barely eked out a bachelor's degree, but you know, she's *very* creative. Wide range of interests—which is one of the *reasons* she barely could get through a bachelor's degree, found it hard to limit herself, which means she is very well rounded. And you know she's on the *radio.*"

"He's such a nice boy." His mother would smile.

"She can do a tongue twister in Hungarian," my father would chime in.

"He's a good listener."

"She can carry a tune."

"He's circumcised."

"Say no more."

And then his parents would give my parents a few chickens, a piece of silk, a few hundred ducats, and a blanket of goosedown, and the deal would be signed as they poured round after round of vodka shots in celebration. The thought of it made my flesh crawl. I mean, you want to make your parents happy, but not *that* happy.

But what choice did I have? We were hundreds of miles from home, he sounded nice enough, he had asked me over for dinner (willing to cook!), and my God, for all I knew he had been sent by the Almighty himself. Now *that* is a dilemma. God finds you the perfect person but it turns out to be a friend of your parents. Do you go, or feign illness and avoid all future contact until he gets the hint? I decided to go.

I went to his house directly from work, and as it happens, he was talking on the phone when I arrived. Now, some people may be put off by a host on the phone who continues to talk for a few minutes after you walk in the door. I saw this as an excellent sign. Not of his manners, necessarily, but it hinted that this man might actually have—dare I say it?—friends.

In general, men don't really have good friends. Certainly not in the same way that women do. Unless they're gay, which is why women and gay men get along so very famously. And it is their lack of friendships that can make straight men act like big possessive anchors tied around your neck. "You told her *that*?!" your boyfriend will say incredulously when you tell him what you and your girlfriends discussed the previous day. "That's private!"

"Honey," you reassure him, "nothing is private between girlfriends. Nothing."

You see, you have girlfriends for every mood. The ones who are wild and will do wild things with you, the ones who are psychologically minded and will overanalyze everything with you, the ones who you go to for reassurance and who never tell you the cold hard truth (which you know they are not telling you), and the ones who will always lay it on the

line, if you are in the mood for that kind of thing. A woman
has to have an array of friends like she does earrings. One for
every mood.

So he seemed to have friends. A good sign. I used the few
minutes of independence while he talked on the phone to look
around his house and scour his bookshelves. The first thing
that struck me was that he actually *had* bookshelves that actually housed books on them (as opposed to last weekend's
empty quarter keg), another good sign. They were crammed
with academic journals, but he had his fair share of fiction,
which I personally found reassuring. The next thing that
caught my eye was that there were things on the wall that were
actually framed. Nicely framed. All together, this made me
wonder if maybe he was gay and his family didn't know. But
then I remembered his glasses, which looked remarkably like
bullet-proof shields, and knew that no gay man in his right
mind would be seen in such atrocities. While not many will
admit it, I think it is fair to say that when one meets a blind
date, one employs a kind of mental stenographer to take notes
of all the positives and negatives of the evening. Things like
"Very cute but needs a new haircut." Or, "Ooh, my parents will
hate him, let's get married." When I walked into Paul's apartment I thought to myself, Bad glasses. Nice legs. (He was
wearing shorts.) The whole feel of the place, of him, was warm
and homey and comfy. I liked it instantly. I could tell that he
was one of the good guys, like a great big comforter, and that
just hit the spot. I knew right away that he was a contender.

He had made dinner, spaghetti of some sort, and that was
fine—a meal that clearly said, "I went to a little more effort
than usual, but nothing that took me more than an extra half
hour or so"—and we of course spent the whole evening trying

to piece together all the zillions of connections we had. The whole evening was spent saying things like "*You* know Lisa Brodkey?" and "*You've* been to Carl's hot-dog stand? On 83rd and South Chicago?!" It was an evening full of exclamation points. I mean, just who was this man who seemed so familiar, so much like kin that sentences hardly needed completing?

We went out a few more times. He got many points for:

- Coming with me to a funky dance club, even though I think even he will admit he has virtually no rhythm and I am a rhythm machine. (While we were dancing, a very tall man dancing next to me leaned over and in a beautiful bass voice said, "You don't want to hurt him, now.")
- Being game for anything.
- Coming with me to see a girlfriend who was visiting from out of town (he knew he was being tested).
- Holding his own at a party.
- Sitting up close at the movies.
- Warming my feet.
- Flossing.
- Being an excellent listener.
- Being nicer than me (*big* points).
- Having been around the block.
- Having cool friends.
- Looking good in a baseball cap (I hate to say it, but if a man doesn't look good in either a baseball cap or a tuxedo, he has a long row to hoe).

He was growing on me. Seeping into my affections. Being with him didn't take a whole lot of mental gymnastics or questioning of my own sanity. There was little to complain about (in and of itself a potential problem with someone like me, but do let's move on). He wasn't Harrison Ford, but I'd chased my fair share of Harrisons and thought I was ready to move on. Or was I?

I evaluated his best and worst qualities. His best quality? He was like *family*. There was so much that didn't need explaining. We had so many things in common. A real security blanket (comforter, in fact) in an otherwise crazy world. His worst quality? He was like *family*. Deadly. El boro. Not a hint of danger anywhere (he had some bow ties in his closet!). It was a real dilemma for a girl like me. And, of course, there was nowhere I could turn for help. I mean, it seemed to even an unreligious person like myself that the big guy had come through. It was like God was actually calling my bluff, bellowing, "You said you wanted a nice guy—well, here he is, so stop complaining, you ingrate!"

He had a point. Did I want to spend the rest of my life chasing misogynist carpenters and arch-conservative assemblymen? Well, of course, part of me did—and always will—but another part of me was beginning to tire of just such antics. Yet I knew myself well, and was all too aware of my natural inclination to feed my most selfish whim. I was tortured by a hesitancy to commit to anything if that meant even the remotest possibility of missing out on something else. Even though he was the greatest. Even though it seemed clear to everyone else. Even though even *I* knew, somewhere in my heart of hearts, that he was it. Admitting it was like pulling my own teeth. He was so normal, it was abnormal. I was the perfect contestant in the *Let's Make a Deal* of love.

"Would yooooouuuuuuuu trade in the loving, solid relationship you have in your hand right now for the chance at something completely different, maybe better but maybe not, behind door number one?"

I hesitate as half the crowd chants, "Take—the—man. Take—the—man," while the other half chants, "Take—the—door. Take—the—door." The emcee comes back at me.

"Ooooooooorrrrrr, would you trade in two blind dates and a guy you really like for the chance at an unknown but stunning man behind door number two?" And I am paralyzed.

You see, the notion that perfection can exist has haunted me forever. But if you believe that there really *is* a man who has the body of a carpenter, the allure of the bad boy, the charisma of a fling, the talent of a Broadway star, the humor of a comic, and the intellect of a Ph.D., all wrapped up in a blanket of stability, then you also believe that all you have to do is look hard enough and wait long enough and the brass ring will be yours for keeps. And so, when Mr. Nice Guy from the Neighborhood Who Was a Friend of the Family was staring me in the face, offering me the best of familylike comfort and the worst of familylike familiarity, I was caught in the dilemma of a lifetime. He offered just about everything a girl is looking for. He offered less of what she fantasized about. He was reality in the best and worst sense. So, after two years of dating, even I secretly knew that something had to be done. So I did something.

I married him.

ALTARED STATES

*The trouble with some women is that they get all
excited about nothing—and then marry him.*

—CHER

OKAY, SO IT WASN'T QUITE
so simple. Everyone loved him instantaneously. What could be
more aggravating than that? Then when you belly up to someone and say, "Can I just tell you how aggravating it can be
when he takes Kleenex and wraps it around his finger and then
proceeds to pick his nose as though nose picking is somehow
made more polite if you swaddle your finger in tissue? I mean
really!" And your friend looks at you and says, "Honey, get
real—call me when you have something substantial, like, he
had an affair with your sister—*then* we can talk! A nice Jewish
boy, with a Ph.D. no less." And I'm thinking, But he looks so
white out there on the dance floor! My friends adored him and
thought any hesitancy I had was preposterous. In fact, after
meeting him in New York (I wasn't there at the time), one of
my very closest friends called me up immediately and summed
up many people's thoughts in four succinct words.

"You don't deserve him!" she shouted at me. And I said to
her, "But those glasses are like bullet-proof shields, they have
to go, don't you think?"

I know I come off as being an incredibly small and shallow person, which of course I am, but things are always different when the life you are passing judgment on is your own. I, too, would have said this man was utterly perfect if someone else were asking me my opinion about him as he related to a potential boyfriend for *her*. But when it's you, you just judge things differently. This is the same reason you get along so well with your girlfriends. You're not sleeping with them. You can let their foibles slide. Any one of their quirks and annoying habits might get to you within five minutes if you were out on a date with them, but the whole beauty of having girlfriends is that you let the really annoying parts of their personalities roll right off you. In fact, you find them sort of funny and endearing. Were your boyfriend to do the exact same thing, you'd want to wring his neck. That is just a law of nature. And, since you are not dating your girlfriends, you have not stated to the world that one of them is the person you will commit the rest of your life to, the *rest of your life* to, her constant tardiness, the way she bites her nails to nubs, her constant hemming and hawing about any little thing, these are *fine* with you, because they do not reflect back on you in any way. No observer is saying to her mate under her breath, "What do you think is wrong with her that she would marry a person who would wear glasses like that?" And of course, that is the biggest irrational fear when you attach yourself to someone. That other people will think that you are like him. Thus, the things you don't love about him get blown way out of proportion and start crowding out the things that you do love about him.

It's like the Jewish-shopper syndrome. Let me explain. When someone compliments me on, say, a shirt I am wearing, it is an impulse beyond my control to blurt out, "Six bucks!" This, I've noticed, is a syndrome. It is the same impulse that responds to every compliment with a negation. Should someone tell me that the meal I just cooked was delicious, I absolutely *have* to say, "It was soooooooo easy, really. It looks much more complicated than it really is." Or, should someone say, "You have beautiful hair," I am compelled to say, "Yeah, and I pay for the beautiful hair on my head by being covered with black, wiry hair all over the rest of me, so be careful what you wish for!" This is too much information for some people. They really only mean well, and it would be so much more gracious just to be able to utter a simple thank you and not drag them through the mud of your personal preoccupations. This is an ailment I've noticed that a lot of my fellow brethren suffer from. It's like the opposite of one-upmanship. It's one-downmanship.

Imagine overhearing a conversation at a Waspy country club that went something like this:

"Lovely tennis set you're wearing today, Libby."

"Oh thank you, Lisette. You know, I got it at Neiman's, but to tell you the truth I really haven't been happy with the quality of their merchandise. I think from now on I'm going to Barneys."

"Oh, I know exactly what you mean. I gave up on Neiman's a long time ago. And Barneys is fine for the everyday, but if you're looking for something special, I go to New York and just drop in on Yves's place and see what they've got."

"Or Paris is always good."

"If you must, but frankly, dear, nothing compares with Milan."

"You are absolutely right about that, I think I'll go have a talk with my travel agent."

Among Jews, the conversation would sound more like this:

"Yoo-hoo, Marcy, come over here right now and tell me where you got that fabulous outfit."

"Loehmann's. Twenty-five bucks on double markdown with my birthday bonus! It has a small hole right here, but who could tell?"

"You know, you might try Syms. They've got a triple-red-dot sale going on. I bought thirteen bras for fifteen dollars. Now *that's* a steal!"

"Don't I know it. See these earrings? Fifty cents at TJ Maxx. I had to glue one back together, but you'd hardly notice it. I hear there's a new place opening up next to Naomi's Nails on Dundee Road. You wanna go?"

"Well, if you want to know the truth, I think you're a much better bargain hunter than me. You have such a good eye for color."

"I was just going to say that I think *you* are the best shopper I know."

"Well, we could give it a try."

"Okay, but let's stop at the Dairy Hut, they have a fabulous soft serve, just twelve calories an ounce."

"Or the Ice Cream Dream, theirs is only ten calories an ounce . . ."

You get the point. Well, it is the same thing with men. A woman comes along and says to me, "You know, you have a fantastic boyfriend," and I find myself saying things like "Yeah, but you should have seen the glasses he used to wear." It's a gut reaction to *have* to point out a flaw.

Any flaw. And if you are mad at him, it's a barrage of flaws. What kind of warped person does this kind of thing? Walk up to any old Jewish couple and this is the likely conversation you will have.

You: "You know, Mrs. Himmelfarb, your husband is really a
    treat. He's smart and funny and he's an excellent lawyer."
Her: "He has terrible gas."
You: "Oh . . . still, though, he is a real treat to have around."
Her: "When he isn't trimming his toenails with his teeth."
You: (tossing off a laugh) "Oh, Mrs. Himmelfarb, you are so
    funny. I'll talk with you at the banquet. I feel so honored to
    be sitting next to Mr. Himmelfarb."
Her: "I hope for your sake he doesn't have a lot of herring."

I don't know from whence it came, I just know that it is hardwired into a whole people. So when I met my future husband, I knew that he was a person of the utmost quality,
integrity, and heart. He took me to great places. New York,
Philly, Baltimore, Paris. He liked walking a city end to end.
Yet he could also be incredibly lazy, like me. And as industri-
ous. Didn't mind going shopping. Or watching movies in
hotel rooms. He ran at my pace on the very few occasions
when we ran together. He didn't laugh at me for constantly
making claims to clean up my eating habits or exercise patterns and failing. He ate anything I cooked and seemed
happy with it. He never said anything about my weight—
reason enough to marry a man! Loved my friends (what's not
to like?). Loved a bargain. Balanced his checkbook to the
penny. He gave me a beautiful antique radio for my birthday,
which we put near the window so we could get Germany and
Japan on the shortwave. He liked camping, also the theater.
He was happy in either a dress-up or dress-down kind of situation. But I just couldn't let it go at the fact that he was great
and life was good.

I had to examine and analyze until he was reduced to so many characteristics lying in a heap on the floor. So imagine just how I felt two years later when, in the parking lot of a fine French restaurant, he asked me to marry him. MARRY HIM. I tried to speak but couldn't. I think I started to blanch. He took one look at me and, being the kind and gentle soul he is, said, "You don't have to say anything right now, you can think about it if you want," and I could feel the blood slowly oozing back into my brain. He could not have read me more clearly. Of course, this was his fatal flaw. He gave me an out and I ran with it. I mean, how many times in your life are you faced with this kind of monumental decision, all hinging on a one-word answer? Say yes and you have committed the rest of your life to one person, this person, who doesn't always clean his ears as well as he should. What if a better ear cleaner should come along and you are already knitting booties? On the other hand, say no and you commit yourself to many more years of dismal dates while you quietly kill yourself for letting the perfect man get away. It was excruciating. The life I'd always wanted lay right within my grasp. And therein lay the rub, that the life I'd always wanted lay right within my grasp. Only a fellow neurotic can understand the problem.

And so, I took the out he offered me. I waited and waited for divine intervention. I waited for a great deity to hurl a thunderbolt into my studio apartment with a little note attached that said either "Do it" or "Forget it," like a celestial eight ball. Nothing appeared. And, for the first and only time in my life, my girlfriends were no good to me. Not that they didn't listen to me harangue endlessly about the pros and cons—they did, with great patience. But this is not something that you can take another person's advice about, and when you are used to doing a fair amount of consulting before you even buy a pair of jeans, it is a lonely road indeed. Because your friends may love him, but they don't have to commit the rest of their lives to him. Or they may understand your fears, at which point you want to sing his praises. Sybil would have an easier time than I did with this decision. I talked to him in the meantime (it wasn't like I closed the curtains, bolted the door, and had food brought in on a tray), but as you can well imagine, there was an underlying awkwardness to the conversations, a proverbial five-billion-pound gorilla in the room at all times.

And so, lonely though it was, I finally made my decision. It took me two weeks. Involved in every decision of this proportion is a leap of faith. I leapt. Then I sent him some flowers with a card that had one word on it: "Yes." But you know, before you think ill of me for making this poor man wait as long as a fortnight for an answer, let me share with you a conversation I once had with a long-lost friend of mine who was catching up with me over the phone and told me she was engaged. Engaged! This was a woman who had told me she never wanted to get married, so I was naturally curious about the turn of events that had led her down this path. She told me the story. Turns out, she and her boyfriend were in the car, on their way out of town for a romantic weekend together, when he out of the blue asked her to marry him.

"That's great," I replied. "Did you say yes?"

"Yes," she said, downheartedly.

"What's the matter?" I asked. "Do you have reservations?"

"Yes," she said, "many, but I just didn't want to ruin the weekend."

Now, this is totally understandable to me. I've known women who've gotten married for lesser reasons than that. I bring this up not to make you think that I entered into my marriage without giving it serious thought, but to illustrate that there is no telling what might be going on in the mind of a girl. Which is, of course, the beauty of the feminine mystique.

TILL DEATH DO US PART

I married beneath me. All women do.
— LADY NANCY ASTOR

EVERYTHING CHANGES
once you decide to get married. Your life is never the same. For one thing, people start treating you differently, relating to you differently. At least they do when you wait as long as I did. I think their sheer relief at getting you "all taken care of" is displayed in a newfound respect. Like, "Hey, she's finally snared a man, she must really *be* somebody, so let's let her into the club." It's absolutely infuriating. The world is definitely divided up into three parts, the single, the engaged, and the married, as though your marital status is the only thing that defines you. When it comes to being single, there is always a little undercurrent of blaming the victim. Well-meaning relatives who lean over at the Thanksgiving table and whisper, "I'm sorry things didn't work out with Bubba, but have you ever thought that maybe you shouldn't be so *picky*?" And what it all comes down to, other than the fact that all parents feel that they don't have to "worry" about their children once they get married, is that in the eyes of potential grandparents, there is nothing like potential progeny. Nothing else will do. You could write the great American

novel, sing at the Met, and win the Nobel prize, and your mother would say, "Nice plaque, dear, but have you ever thought about a dating service?"

And once you do decide to get married, you open yourself up to a torrent of torture. Total strangers think they are your friends and relatives, and your friends and relatives start acting like total strangers. I knew one woman who felt that her own mother became a complete stranger to her when her mother couldn't be swayed from planning an extravagant wedding at the Plaza in New York with a twenty-four-piece band. Previously they had gotten along famously. This maneuver made the daughter see a side of her mother that was completely new to her, and she felt estranged, put off, and sort of disgusted by it. So the daughter and her fiancé went down to City Hall and got married in secret. Then she went ahead with the mother's wedding six weeks later, never telling a soul. She said that she was much more relaxed knowing that she was already married and had a much better time at her wedding than she would have otherwise. I thought that was brilliant. Weddings are fertile soil for unrealistic expectations, parental takeovers, and dashed hopes, all at about four or five thousand bucks an hour, so whatever you can do to make yourself happy at your own wedding is completely kosher as far as I'm concerned.

Anyone and everyone comes up to you and gives you unsolicited advice. Anyone. It's like you woke up one day in the middle of an Ann Landers column with a hundred collective voices saying things like "Listen, hon, marriage is great, but it's tough. The first year is the worst. Don't go to bed mad (I'd never go to bed!), never say never, and don't expect your husband to be your girlfriend. You'll be fine. If not, get counseling."

And it just seems to escalate from there. Paul and I went to see the rabbi who was to marry us, and in the middle of a lighthearted shmooze, he looked right at me and said, "I was worried about you, Gwen, I thought that emotionally, you might price yourself right out of the market." I need to hear this? From a rabbi yet? There is absolutely nothing more infuriating than someone who gets right to the heart of the matter in the space of, say, a sentence or two. How did he know that I tend to suffer from an extreme form of self-confidence (no one is good enough for me) undermined by gross insecurity (no one could ever love me)? I barely even knew the guy. And he had to say it in front of the fiancé? I might as well just have been naked and hanging by my toes for all the protection I had in that room that day.

People don't relate to you anymore as Gwen. Now, you are Gwen, the Soon-to-Be-Married Person. This status is completely horrifying to the proud Single Person. Some women love it, of course, and more power to them, since this just means more Prozac for me. But it is as if there is a group, maybe a cult even, that is about to accept you as a member, and they are just so happy about it, it's sort of creepy. And once you are a member, they can all breathe a collective sigh of relief, brush you aside as someone they no longer have to worry about, and move on to the next prospective applicant.

For my own wedding, I knew what I didn't want: bridesmaid dresses, bouquet throwing, garters, and a bachelorette party. (My sister's bachelorette party was a dark escapade I didn't want to repeat. We went to a usually all-male bathhouse that reserved Wednesday nights for women. We signed up for massages. I envisioned LaCosta Spa. Instead, I was directed, nude, to a room that could only be described as a replica of the gas chamber at Dachau. A huge room with nothing but one table and dozens of shower heads. Not a soul was there. At the far end of the room there was a wooden door. I tiptoed up to it and peeked in. It was a sauna, and the little window in the door was too steamy to see inside. I ventured in. There, like a living Diane Arbus photo, was one older, gigantic, naked woman reaching into a bucket of branches and flogging another older, gigantic, naked woman with eucalyptus leaves. Steam exploded off the rocks and swirled to the ceiling. One of the gigantic women looked at me and motioned for me to go. I did so promptly. She clearly was not a native English speaker. She evenually stepped out of the sauna, still naked, and motioned for me to follow. I didn't feel I had a choice. Then she motioned for me to get up on the one table in the middle of the gas chamber. I suddenly understood that she was the masseuse. I prayed she had some kind of frock hidden away somewhere that she planned to put on before she began the massage. I was wrong. She threw me around that table like she was kneading a Christmas Stollen. At one point, her mighty breasts, which closely resembled sandbags in size and weight, completely enveloped my face and I was actually fighting for air. I'll stop there. Needless to say, I never forgave my sister.) I knew what I did want: music, lots of friends, a very cool dress.

We got married in the middle of one of the worst snowstorms Chicago had seen in years. Fourteen inches the day before the wedding. But at the same time the streets were absolutely sparkling and it made the whole thing seem like we were getting married inside of a snow globe. The invitations were cassettes (once a radio producer, always a radio producer), the dress was a very sheer silk number I picked up at a craft show, and the reception was at a brewery. The actual ceremony took place at a synagogue where we sang, lit candles, walked with our families down the aisle, and both stomped on glasses wrapped in napkins to shouts of "Mazel Tov!" Then we moved on to the brewery, where we shimmied late into the night and then went out for hot dogs at 3 A.M. because no one eats at their own wedding. While I might've been nervous for the two years preceding the wedding, I wasn't nervous in the slightest on the day of. Nothing like a great big party, I always say.

But like any other much-anticipated event, a wedding comes and goes all too quickly. A few pictures, a few flowers, a little salmon, and the deed is done, the knot is tied. The sun rises and sets and the world still turns. All that planning, all that worrying, and it's over. And then, slowly, the stark realization starts setting in. The guests go home, the music stops, and the doors are locked. And there you are, faced with a brand-new situation in a dress you'll never wear again with a man who will have to see you expelling the afterbirth. But don't worry if you feel suddenly panicky, it's only for the next fifty years or so. That much-talked-about, much-analyzed part of your life that happens after you take off the last tablecloth, fold the last folding chair, and slip out of your dress and into your jeans. It's called the aftermath.

PART 3

FROM HERE
TO MATERNITY
crossing the monumental divide

Today is the first day of the wreck of your life.
—BECKY BURKE

YOU DON'T HAVE TO BE EVEL KNIEVEL TO CROSS A monumental divide, just a girl with a lot of moxie and stamina. Which perfectly describes a girl like you. That's what it took to get you here and that's what it'll take to keep you going. I mean, getting to the place where you can think about marriage isn't as complicated as it seems. After all, marriage is really the same as dating, it's just that when you get to the breakup part, you don't. That, plus the F word, as in "forever." And anything that lasts forever has to be mighty resilient to withstand the rigorous wear and tear it will have to weather. But you are just the kind of girl to tackle such a daring ride on love's roller coaster, now that you've taken all the time you needed to get over the commitment thang.

And daring you are. Who else in their right mind would voluntarily enter into a legal arrangement by which you must talk to, listen to, and look at the same person for the next, say, forty or fifty years? Really, it's unimaginable. But here we are. Let's make the best of it.

What my generation really wants to know is: Why didn't anyone tell us it was going to be *this* hard? Why didn't someone tell us that training a husband was a full-time job, that you'd work your whole life to have a career that you would then have to leave at its height if you wanted to procreate, that procreating might be dependent on the bank account of the Sultan of Brunei and a romance with a turkey baster, and that you might never sneeze without peeing again? Why didn't anyone tell me years ago that I just *might* not have the time to do things like act on Broadway, become a midwife, teach, build a house with my bare hands, travel the world, save the world, marry ten men — and maybe a woman or two — write the great American novel, join the Peace Corps, get a black belt, bear eight children, and become the fourth Pointer sister? How was I supposed to know that I would go to bed one night worried about whether I could buy a pair of Earth Shoes or not and wake up the next morning worried about the other F word, as in "forty"? And "fifty"?

Brace yourself, 'cause here's the bad news (and believe me, Toots, it's not like me to shove reality in your face, but I feel I must be brutally honest here): They *did* tell us. Over and over and over again. Collectively, we just happened to be like your average second-grader walking around with our hands in our ears, singing "nya, nya, nya, nya, nya" to ourselves. They told us that it is hard, they printed divorce statistics, they warned us not to pay attention to the media images of perfect relationships. They also showed us by way of example. Our parents screamed and yelled at each other, our friends' parents screamed and yelled at each other, and then people our own age who dared to get married started screaming and yelling at each other. At least in the worlds I traveled in. (But then again, I am a hothead — see the following pages — and everyone I know and respect is a hothead, so perhaps there is another way out there, but I don't know a thing about it. Go ask a Protestant.)

They told us, but we refused to listen. Rather than look at the evidence staring us in the face every day and say to ourselves, "Hmmmm, this marriage-and-parenthood thing looks awfully challenging, perhaps I will mentally prepare myself for such an ordeal by embarking on some extensive reality training so that I will not be obsessed with all the disappointments ahead of me," we just look at those who've come before us and say to ourselves, "Hmmm, they must've just really fucked up. We will do better," and skip merrily down the road to ruin.

Every single person on this earth, with the exception of those so well balanced you want to wring their necks, thinks (or at least hopes and prays) that she can do a better job than her parents and everyone in her parents' generation. We have to, otherwise no one in their right mind would get married and have babies and the species would die out and cockroaches would rule the world. This is part of our hard wiring. Survival of the species. This is why so many people who are estranged from their families nevertheless go out and start their own (this is also why therapists have summer homes). They see themselves as superior in some way until a few years and a few kids in, when they realize that their parents weren't dark and twisted depressives who delighted in torturing each other and giving their children complexes; they were, in fact, damned impressive, shining examples of patience and perseverance in the tortuous vortex you have come to know as marriage and parenthood. I know one woman who had twins—a boy and a girl—and as soon as the girl came out she reached for the phone and called her mother in tears, crying, "I'm sorry for everything I ever did to you!"

Such is the cycle of life.

I see it as my job — nay, my responsibility — to make sure that you know what you are in for when you call the caterer and let the expiration date on your Ortho jelly go by. But I actually think my wise sister expressed it best when she told me, "You know, I think of myself as a highly emotional person, but I have never known such depths of love and hate until I got married and had children." What more is there to be said? Just a few things, which is why I am here. If you are already stuck there, you will at least know you have company. And if you're on your way, you won't feel slighted or unprepared once you get there. So now you can move forward, read on, and for God's sake, get those fingers out of your ears.

THE BEIGE SUIT

My grandmother was a very tough woman. She buried
three husbands. Two of them were just napping.
— RITA RUDNER

EVERY MAN HAS AT <u>LEAST</u>
one piece of clothing that is not only unflattering, outdated,
and frankly hideous, but also reveals much about his nonexistent sense of style and fashion, to say nothing of his misguided
self-image. Either that or he is just too oblivious to notice how
bad he looks all the time. Now, a man who is officially color
blind has an excuse to be seen in seersucker. But unless he has
a note from his doctor, forget it. Where most men fall through
the cracks is in thinking that if it was fashionable once, it is
always worthy of wear. Their requirements of a piece of clothing are dangerously simple. It has to fit. Or have fit at one
time, like sophomore year of high school—that alone entitles
said garment to at least ten more years of wear.

I am not above keeping things for years and years. Much
of my wardrobe has turned into Kleenex from so much wear
and tear. But these are inoffensive items. Basics. Things that
never were in high style and will never go out of style. Jeans
and T-shirts. I do not keep gauchos in my closet simply because
they looked good on me in 1976. Men do not understand this

concept, unless, of course, they are gay or architects. And gay architects? *Come sit by me, honey.* (My father would be the one exception to this rule. Though he is an architect, and can build monoliths that tower over mankind, he cannot match a shirt and tie to save his life. The style of his suits and ties—which he just buys duplicates of once they wear out—makes him look like he should be carrying a violin case and breaking kneecaps. All he's missing is the spats. Needless to say, this drives my mother, who does have taste, to fits of rage and despair. Finally, after close to fifty years of marriage, she is wearily waving the white flag. This could be you if you're not careful. So let us revise this gross generality to *young* architects. No offense, Dad.) But your run-of-the-mill guy? A walking fashion don't. And a woman who is thinking about any involvement whatsoever with the run-of-the-mill guy would do well to look into his closet before taking any plunge whatsoever. Even for the most minimal of commitments. Like lunch.

No woman I know needs much prompting to rattle off the items of clothing that her partner owns or used to own (before she got hold of it) that she hates most intensely. I'm not talking about minor irritation, a thorn in one's side, a petty embarrassment in a room full of friends. I'm talking about an item of clothing that brings your blood to a roiling boil and makes your heart beat in your chest like a kettledrum. If you were to walk into a party with your partner who had selected for the evening, say, a pair of plaid pants, a checked tie, and a polka-dotted shirt, no one else would think a thing of it. In fact, they might even think it a little charming, saying to themselves, "That Ralph, what an unusual dresser he is . . . goofy, but we love him." But inside you want to stand up and

yell to the whole gathering, "I just want to announce right
now that I had nothing to do with this man's outfit. He was
wearing it when he picked me up, I know that it is hideous,
and frankly, it disgusts me so much that I would rather be
home popping a boil than be out with someone who would
dress this way. I want nothing to do with him, so please, people, don't associate me with any part of this miscreant you see
before you—I am *begging* you!" But of course you do not have
the nerve to address the whole crowd at once, so you just
spend the evening whispering into the ears of your good
friends, "I had nothing to do with it, please forgive me," even
though they had not given it a second thought. If it were one
of their dates, that would be a different matter entirely.

For me, it was Paul's beige suit. No one on the planet
looks good in a beige suit. No one. And since Paul already has
a beige complexion when he doesn't live in a tropical climate,
which is never, beige is not really his best color. Naturally, he
doesn't know this, and bought a suit that would test even
Nancy Reagan's idea of bland. And it's not *the* most godawful
thing I've ever seen, but it just *gets* me right where I live. Especially in the winter, when the last color you want reflecting
back up at your face is a beige of any kind, taupe, ecru,
eggshell, wheat, sand, buck, tan, or café au lait included. And,
I might add, this suit is ill fitting. It has little pleats that pull
instead of lie flat, there is no tie in the world that goes with it,
and it is a complete waste of the poor cotton plant that gave its
very blossom for the cause. I despise it. And when he wears it,
I despise him. I can't help it. When he comes in after dressing
in the morning and I see that he is wearing the beige suit, I
want to shoot him dead. It just puts me in a bad mood for the
rest of the day. A *really* bad mood. There is nothing he can say

that will make me like him any more at that moment. I am wildly distracted by my hatred of that suit, and thereby him, until he has taken it off at the end of the day and put it away out of my eyesight.

Now, maybe you don't have such strong feelings about an article of clothing that isn't even yours. How can I explain it to you? Well, it would be what an old friend of mine used to call a ping. Only this would be bigger than a ping, like a PING. Or a PEEENG. A ping is the little something that a person says or does in the course of getting to know him that hits you upside the head and makes you say to yourself, "Ping! I don't like men who drink beer from undergarments." Like maybe he tells you he voted for Reagan. Ping! Or maybe he tells you he is really married. Big PING! Or maybe he just picked the movie without consulting you or doesn't wear his seat belt. Ping! Ping! It's like watching the lemons register on your mental slot machine as he tries to impress you by sending up what he thinks will be cherries.

Everyone has to deal with a certain number of pings, since, unfortunately, no one is pingless, but everyone must also judge for themselves just how many pings they can stand before bolting. Fashion pings may ring louder for some women than for others. Some women really don't care, and more power to them, since they will have their pick of virtually millions of men—go, girl! But for the rest of us, the fashion ping is serious.

Of course, there are only so many things you can expect from a man, and certainly taste isn't one of them. The story of Paul buying the suit is a tragic tale repeated millions of times every day all over the world. It goes like this: Man goes into clothing store, looks at suits, is immediately overwhelmed, grabs the first few on the rack, tries them on to see if they fit, and, provided they don't have three legs, buys them. He goes to the shirt department and buys white shirts (classic but boring—and that reflection thing again) or white shirts with red or blue stripes or even worse, a blue shirt with a white *collar*. Then, without even a hint of a memory for what he just bought moments ago, he moves to the tie department and just picks some out for reasons that escape me completely. Probably because they are the cheapest ones there. Or the closest to him. Then he gathers everything together and walks out with not one item that goes with another. My eyes well up just thinking about it. Paul was no different. I asked him why he bought the suit.

"I don't know." He shrugged.

Ask the same question of a woman and she will tell you, "Well, the auburn pants I bought when I was feeling really bad about myself one day and decided to get myself a treat. The print dress was when I had just lost some weight, and I can't even fit into the thing now, but I keep it around to try on every once in a while to see just how far I am from being that thin again. These black pants are my old faithfuls; I can fit into them no matter what I weigh since they have elastic in the back of the waistband and drop pleats in the front, creating give in the back and a slimming effect in the front, a perfect combination. And the mustard blouse was the best thing I ever did, on sale at Loehmann's, plus I had a thirty-percent-off coupon so I got it for under ten bucks—Escada, no less—no ironing, goes in the machine. Who knew I could get away with such a color?"

I feel the need to explain here that the male fashion ping does not extend to the grubby in my case. To me, grubby is sexy. Not grubby as in a shirt that hasn't been washed in a year or two, but grubby as in oversized, tattered, faded—I love that. I mean, what girl in her right mind didn't think that the "Dud" was by far the cutest guy in the game Mystery Date? The surfer? Get real. The Dud *had* it and was the one I secretly lusted after. And what was he wearing? A pair of baggy khaki pants and a rumpled white shirt half untucked. Now that is an outfit for the ages. Always in fashion, always sexy. So I don't get riled over old baggy sweatshirts that are torn and faded; I love those, and usually stole them from boyfriends whenever I could. But it is different to see a man in something that he thinks looks fine and you know looks terrible, like a brown pair of pants, a blue shirt, and a red tie. When Paul comes into the room dressed like this, I stare at him and say, "Can I just ask you a question? What the hell were you thinking when you got dressed this morning?" and he says with complete sincerity, "What?" and looks down at himself wondering what is wrong.

"What made you choose that red tie, for instance?"

"This tie? I don't know, it was the first one I grabbed."

"So, that is your criterion? If it's hung up, then it goes with everything?"

"Well, doesn't it?"

At this point it was all I could do to not walk out the door and headlong into the ocean.

"Have you ever given any thought to colors that match, hues that are alike, and clothes that actually go together?"

"Not really."

And that explains many a mystery about the opposite sex. It confirms their wanton obliviousness, their lack of any eye for detail, and their complete aesthetic failure, among other things. It is also a disappointing blow that illustrates the difference between what you *thought* he knew about himself and what turns out to be complete and total lack of self-awareness. It speaks volumes.

Some people say that you shouldn't judge a man by the way he dresses, but clearly, these people are men. Any woman with blood running through her veins will tell you otherwise. Some men may dress poorly as a gesture of defiance. You know, "I am not going to give in to the ridiculous trends that drive the capitalist marketplace, nor will I prostitute myself to the world of overpriced ideas of what someone else says I should wear." This at least I can respect, even though I often feel like saying, "Okay, but how 'bout just for tonight?" But it is the rare man who is using his 1973 wardrobe as a political protest, so you have to put your rage in simple terms. When he puts on the beige suit, you look at him and say to yourself, It is so obvious to me that what you are wearing makes you look like you've been lying in a drawer for a few months with a tag on your toe, I fail to see how it could *not* be obvious to you. And you begin to wonder about the very fabric of marriage that you have woven and how it could be unraveling so (hopefully the fabric is not beige).

If you are lucky, you may end up with a man who is "trainable," a term a friend of mine finds extremely distasteful but one which I happen to adore. She thinks it connotes that the man has no opinions and would kowtow to a woman's preferences. Exactly, I say. What could be better than that? The more trainable the better. We need men of opinions, especially men of the opinion that women know better when it comes to dressing them. That is an ideal man. Paul has reluctantly agreed to leave behind the beige suit, since he also agrees that I have far better taste than he does. One day he wore something I'd given him and came home from work in a daze, saying, "This is the first time I've ever gotten a compliment on a single thing I've worn. *Ever.*" When it continued to happen, but only with clothes I'd bought or picked out, he reluctantly agreed that I had better taste, and when the women in his office looked at him and said, "I like that tie you're wearing; Gwen bought it for you, didn't she?" he started begging me to shop with him. He agreed to get rid of the beige suit, finally, but, like buying a shoe rack so his shoes don't spill out of every closet like so many footprints-on-the-floor directions to doing the cha-cha, he hasn't done it yet. He claims he can't get rid of it until he replaces it with another suit, which he has no time to shop for (but given his shopping methods, I like to point out, it would only take two or three minutes). So it is still in his repertoire despite all his promises to dispose of it. I secretly dream of burning that beige suit, and one day, I might. On the other hand, why burn a perfectly good piece of clothing when you could give it away and have it haunt another perfectly nice, unsuspecting woman? In the meantime, maybe once every week and a half, he and his beige suit walk in to say good-bye in the morning and it is all I can do to hold down my breakfast. He just laughs to himself, looks at me calmly, and says, "You hate me right now, don't you?" And I have to be honest.

"Yes, I do. But it's all because of the beige suit."

"Can't you ever separate me from this stupid suit?"

"Not as long as you dress yourself, no." And then he just smiles and shakes his head and walks away, wondering how, with my obsessive attention to detail and deep-seated annoyance over so many minuscule things, I can actually survive even one full day on earth as we know it. If I only knew.

HOTHEADS

Who lit the fuse on your tampon?

—BUTTON

THE BEIGE-SUIT STORY MAY have you thinking ill of me. Petty, you are saying to yourself, nit-picking, and completely unreasonable. To which I can only say, how very astute you are. I am indeed all those things. But, in my own defense, I will tell you that I come from a long line of hotheads. Women chromosomally predispositioned to wanton bitchiness. Before me comes a string of matriarchs whose tempers flared up like the flames of hell. We work at the speed of cyanide, leaving as many survivors in our wake. We're one-woman minefields: Step one foot in the wrong direction and you're likely to get a limb blown off.

Like the weather atop Mount Everest, the moods of a Macsai woman are life-threateningly unpredictable. Sunny one minute, fatal the next. Suffice it to say that when any one of us is in a mood, you would rather look for your contact lens on the autobahn than cross our path.

This is clearly a family trait passed down on the X chromosome. We Macsai women all have the same hair trigger. And yet, the women in my family have managed to beat the odds and stay married for forty-nine years (parents), twenty-two years (sister), fifteen years (sister), fifteen years (brother), and five years (me). How, you may ask, is this possible? Easy. My mother, sisters, and I all married the same kind of man: the oblivious kind. They come in slightly different packages, but underneath their minor surface differences they have one common denominator. They are totally out of it.

Or they can be. You see, keeping up with the whizzing, ricocheting thought patterns of the female Macsai brain can be an exhausting task, one that most men would just walk away from. And what good are they to us anyway? Pish, that's what. Since we have little more tolerance than your average post-coital praying mantis, human males, in the face of such a futile job, just check out.

Now, my father would have to be held up as the king of oblivion, a man whose house could be burning down around him and he would happily just bumble over to the thermostat, lower it, and be happy to be saving on his heating bills. At moments of blinding clarity, the most you can get out of him is an admission of just how oblivious he can be. Not in the details of his own life, of course. In that he is a complete compulsive. The arrangement in which he stores his personal effects in his bureau drawer has not changed in thirty-five years. The toenail clippers are on the far left in a tattered brown leather case; his polishing cloth, folded lengthwise, comes next; then the two watches he doesn't wear; an extra ribbon watchband for when the one he uses wears out; a few keys that he doesn't carry with him; and on the far right, his least-often-used credit cards in a box exactly credit-card-sized. He has only had two hairstyles his whole life: Boris Karloff and Ted Koppel. (He went from Brylcreem to the blow-dryer. Now, instead of having each hair in place by way of grease, he has each hair in place by way of hot air and hair spray, applied at 6:03 A.M. precisely.) His books sit on the library shelves categorized by subject and author, with the spine of one book matching up exactly with the spine of the book next to it. He takes the same shirts to the same laundry every Saturday at exactly seven-thirty, and woe to the unsuspecting relative who, for whatever reason, may be parked behind him in the driveway. This is a man who once confessed to me that if he has a list of six things to do and he happens to complete a seventh, he will write it down on the list, just for the pure satisfaction of crossing it off.

But that is in his own life, where everything is just so and God help the poor grandchild who innocently takes the tracing paper off his drawing board to make a tutu for her dolly. The gasket he would blow when we would clip our teenage toenails and forget to put the clippers back on the far-left-hand side of his top dresser drawer was nothing short of impressive. Otherwise, he just puts on his Mr. Magoo glasses and ignores half of what is happening around him. He can be sitting right next to you at the dinner table when you mention that you and your husband have had a terrible fight and are going to get divorced, and five minutes later, while someone else is in the middle of a sentence, he will turn to you and say, "So, Gwen, how's Paul?" (We recently begged him to have his hearing checked because he was turning the TV up to Lollapalooza levels and saying "What?" all the time. The doctor told him his hearing was fine, which proved my point exactly. His powers of checking out of the room and checking in to oblivion are so great he appears deaf.)

Now the oblivious man (as a collective group) is not as rare as you might think. In fact, I would have to venture a theory that obliviousness is a dominant male gene carried along the Y chromosome. This gene is responsible for a myriad of characteristics like the fact that men really *do* know how to clean a room just as well as women do; the problem is, they just never *notice* that it's dirty. If they did, certainly, they would take it upon themselves to clean it. Really, they would. And it's not that they have any personal aversion to replacing the rancid, mildewed kitchen sponge that has been sitting next to the faucet for a year or two, it's just that they never *notice* that the kitchen smells like there is a dead body under the sink. Otherwise surely they would be on that smell like a bloodhound, inspecting every possible culprit until the house smelled like a spring bouquet (not to mention properly wringing out the sponge so that it doesn't get mildewed in the first place).

This is every woman's curse. Some are able to laugh it off. But I don't know anyone like that. In fact, all the women I know worth their salt are hotheads, like me. We're like an underground cult. We stick together and have regular meetings where we rant and rave and howl at the moon about the most recent idiotic thing that our fathers, brothers, in-laws, cousins, nephews, and, most of all, partners did. A typical exchange between the women in my family may entail a soft opening lob like this:

"Hey, girl, how you doing?"

"How am I doing? I *hate* my goddamned husband. *That's* how I'm doing. He is such a fucking *idiot*. I'd like to wring his neck, the *asshole*."

This kind of exchange doesn't even phase us. In my family, it's the equivalent of "Fine, how are you?" We understand completely and we never take it too seriously. I mean, the crisis is serious at the moment, but these moments come and go so often with women like us, they are nothing to get alarmed about. And we are the perfect people to call when you are feeling hateful, because there is no ugly, gangrenous feeling that we haven't had, so there is no need to be embarrassed. There is nothing worse than being in a complete venomous snit and calling the wrong person.

HOTHEAD: "He is such a shit. I can't stand the sight of him and every little hair on his head makes me want to gouge his eyes out."

WRONG PERSON: "Oh my God, that sounds horrible . . . I've never heard anyone so unhappy. Maybe you should, I don't know . . . um . . . think about a divorce?"

RIGHT PERSON (FELLOW HOTHEAD): "Don't I know it, honey! Half the time I just want to take my husband, slit him down the middle, and stomp on his entrails. Pull his chest hairs out one at a time. Sometimes I feel like if I don't put his gonads into the Cuisinart and pulse, pulse, pulse, I'm just going to explode!"

Now *that* is a girlfriend—or, if you're lucky, a sister.

I've never been quite sure which came first, the hotheaded woman or the oblivious man. Did one trait actually *cause* the other—I mean, if you have to live with a hothead, does obliviousness develop as a necessary survival technique, and vice versa? Or is this simply the only partnership that allows both to coexist with any success whatsoever? An interesting question. It was with this question in mind that I once decided to take the bull by the horns and look in my own backyard to see just what inspired my parents to stay together over the course of almost five decades.

I found my father peacefully sitting in his backyard one afternoon, leaning over a watercolor he was painting. It was a spectacularly beautiful summer day. I decided to join him. We got to talking and I asked him point blank, "Dad, in all the years you've been married, have you ever thought about getting divorced?"

Without missing a beat, or even looking up from his painting, he said, "Every day."

I thought about this momentarily and decided it was only fair at this point to ask the same question of my mother to see what she had to say on the subject. I found her in the kitchen.

"Mom, how come you and Dad never got divorced?" I asked her.

"What, and trade in his problems for somebody else's? No thank you. At least with your father I know what I'm dealing with."

Which perfectly illustrates how the dynamics of the long-term hotheaded woman–oblivious man combination work. It's a combination of resignation, apathy, and the strange interlocking of needs and fulfillment. My father once told me he actually misses it when no one picks on him. Can you think of anything sweeter?

This way of life is not for everyone, however. I had friends in high school who walked into our bickering household and were horrified by the barbs flying back and forth. They didn't last long. They didn't have the central requisite understanding that in a Jewish home, bickering is like an ethnic form of affection. In fact, we as a people have elevated it to an art form. This is why the best sayings and curses are in Yiddish ("He moves like a fart in brine"). And being the best in the world at arguing and putdowns, one wonders just how much we can do to fight our God-given talents. Do we really want to end up eating lutefisk or wearing Top-Siders without socks just to avoid a good, hearty confrontation? If you've ever tasted lutefisk, you'd know the answer is no. So, I say, embrace your hotheadedness. Throw trinkets at the moon in celebration as you link arms with your sisters and vow to nurture these energies. Like Mozart, think of yourself as a vessel, through which the wrath of God is passed. Don't try and bend yourself like a pretzel to be like the martini-lunch-at-the-tennis-club set. Remember: At our weddings there may never be enough to drink, but at theirs there is never enough to eat. Which would you rather have? Let that be your guiding light.

And if it gets to the point where you just have to blow a gasket, erupt like Old Faithful, combust in a rage of biblical proportions, feel free. It is your birthright as a hothead. When it gets to the point that it is too much even for you, you have but one alternative. Call another hothead.

And if she isn't home, call my sister.

BIOLOGICAL WARFARE

*In August, my husband and I celebrated our thirty-eighth
anniversary. You know what I finally realized? If I had
killed him the first time I thought about it, I'd have been
out of jail by now.*

—ANITA MILNER

WHEN YOU DO CALL MY
sister, she will tell you—after talking you out of slipping
cyanide into his morning tea—that it takes a long time to
train a husband. Years, at least—sometimes decades, and
then, by the time you're through, let's face it, the only thing
that's hardening is his arteries. These are the years that you
spend in an endless, annoying, ridiculous pattern.

It goes like this: he doesn't notice that every time you go out
of the house you spend a half an hour getting everyone into
their snowsuits; making sure you have snacks and diapers and
water and Kleenex and wipes and pacifiers and crayons and
extra clothes for when they poop through the clothes they're in,
and keys and wallet and grocery list and tax returns to mail;
then hoisting two children, a stroller, a backpack for when they
get antsy in the stroller, a diaper bag the size of a steamer
trunk, and a doll or two onto your hips; and then collapsing in
a sweaty heap in the car. And instead of thinking to himself,

Hmmmm, I never knew that my wife was half sherpa, perhaps I will relieve her load, he, in the worst-case scenario, never notices and has to be asked a thousand times for help, at which point he begins to resent it and feels like you are nagging (having put you in the position to have to remind him over and over again) or, in a better-case scenario, will say, "What can I do to help you?" which sounds good except that it is at ten-thirty at night, long after your sleep-deprived, badly sprained body has completely shut down. This earns him the brownie points of wanting to be helpful, but absolves him of any actual responsibility. Another one that I like is "Look, I cleaned the kitchen and you didn't even notice! You know, once in a while I would like a little appreciation." And you look around the kitchen, which still has loose items all over the counter that are not washed, three-day-old grime coating the sink, and two pots from dinner still soaking because they are going to be really hard to clean, so, of course, these he will leave up to you. And your decision then is whether to start World War III by saying what you really feel like—"I didn't notice because this kitchen is still not *clean,* as in filthy, and if you had even one eye in your head you would *know* that!"—or admit that instead of having one child you really have two, saying, "Gee, honey, that sure is great! I really like the way you got so much accomplished without being asked. I am so proud of you. Would you like some teddy grahams?"

My husband has often said to me, "You know, I am better than ninety-nine percent of the men out there at _____" (fill in the blank). To which I always say, "And those are your standards?" If I compared myself to the snake's belly of common denominators, I think I'd come out smelling like a rose too. Gather a group of women together anywhere, anytime, and you will inevitably hear the phrase "They just don't get it. They never will." And no matter how much you try to talk, cajole, convince, or argue about certain things, it is true that they just don't get it and never will. A friend of mine recently said that having a husband is like having a really bad assistant that you can't fire. So you train and train and train until they get it right. You continue to put things at the bottom of the stairs in the hope that he will see them and carry them up, even though, without fail, every evening the things are still waiting for you and only you to take up (he would surely take them up, if only he *noticed* they were there).

You threaten to get him a seeing-eye dog if he askes you "Where are the _____?" (fill in the blank) one more time. This amazes me constantly. First, they ask without looking, as though they have just now, for the first time ever, walked into the room they've lived in for maybe twelve years or so. Then, when you swallow your mounting anger, you say, "Look in the drawer to the left of the sink." They open the drawer, look at it, and close it again, saying, "It's not there. Where else can it be?" And you say, "I'm sure it is there, I saw it in there yester-day," and he says, "It's *not* there," so you get up from the dio-rama you are putting together out of Cheerios and pipe cleaners for your kid's school, march over to the drawer, open it, move something to the left, and expose the item he was looking for so pathetically half-assedly, trying desperately to squash the urge to ram it down his throat. I have one friend whose husband nearly got his head cut off when, on a trying day, he asked her casually, "Where are the towels?" (Gee, I don't know, dear, try the oven.)

A personal favorite of mine is when, despite numerous requests to do differently, he still puts wineglasses on their side to dry so that the water gathers in a little pool on the inside of the glass and leaves unsightly rings as it evaporates, which must be removed before using because, after all, glass is see-through. I can hear you now saying "At least he washed it!" to which I can only respond, "Raise your standards, honey!" You are probably shaking your head, saying to yourself, "This girl needs a job!" which I have to admit might be true. Spending too much time at home will cause you to obsess about the teensiest things. However, the wineglass thing is still infuriating. We could surely go on like this for volumes, but let's stop here. In training a husband, all you can do is hope for the best. Hope that some of the pointers you've so gently offered him sink in; hope that he miraculously begins to think like you; hope that you are called away for something excruciatingly important so that he has to take time off work and stay home for, say, a year or two to see what it's really like day after day; or just hope that he still thinks you're cute when you're mad.

THE GREAT DIVIDE

God could not be everywhere and therefore he made mothers.

—JEWISH PROVERB

PEOPLE NATURALLY FALL into various categories. You've got your fellow hotheads, your sisters, your creative types, your stereotypes, your wealthy folk, your florists, short-order cooks, people over six feet, people under psychiatric care, and, of course, the Shriners. And no matter how they are categorized, by job, interests, physical attributes, socioeconomic position, age, or number of face-lifts, the very commonality in each group builds instant camaraderie. You may eavesdrop on a group of architects talking about the pressure per square inch that an I-beam can bear, or what a renowned egotist Frank Lloyd Wright was. Perhaps when you see two strangers talking in an animated fashion about the joys of acidophilus, you can conclude that both are frequent yeast-infection sufferers, or maybe you just see two guys in fezzes talking about where to change the oil in their minicars. Every category bears its own language, its own social system, its own clubbiness that is hard to penetrate if you do not belong.

As a general rule, however, women are able to transcend many such categorizations due to a greater overriding commonality: their femaleness. It trumps the fact that a piano teacher may find herself in the company of an astrophysicist, a caterer, a surgeon, a paralegal, a saleswoman, and a contortionist. And this bond, this vital connection, is so basic, so fundamental, that it is one of the only absolutely reliable, utterly stable things in your whole life, ever.

Until it isn't. There isn't a lot that can separate woman from woman, friend from friend (as long as one is not a GWG), but there is one thing that stands out as coming damn close on many an occasion. And that, of course, is the Big Kahuna. What we are loved for, hated for, revered for, and blamed for. The saintly, the devilish, the very nucleus of life itself: motherhood (and, by extension, child rearing—see future chapters). Motherhood can divide the closest of friends, and it is a testament to motherhood's very intensity that it can have that great an affect on an otherwise unaffectable relationship. But what about marriage, you say? Is there not a great chasm between the hitched and the single? Of course there is. But not as big a chasm, since we've all dated men, and that alone is enough to provide us with a lifetime of stories to regale one another with. Just because some of us were silly enough to marry one or two of them does not take away from our common experience, thus re-forming the bond temporarily severed by some expensive flowers strewn about a church, a piece of soggy chicken cordon bleu, and a gift you know they'll return.

But motherhood is a different matter entirely. It is the one experience, the one condition, the one way of life that forms a natural separation, even a great divide. I mean, how utterly boring is it to hang out with mothers of young children when you are single and childless? Completely and totally. You can feign interest in nipple confusion for only so long. How intensely would you like to strangle the next person who starts a sentence with "Just wait till *you* have kids, you'll see . . ." as she pries her child's toe out of Green Thumb Barbie's mini—watering can, in which it is stuck? And how often would a mother like to be able to have, for one measly little hour in the day, the life of a single person so that she can do something like pick her nose by herself? Every day. And if she is the first one of her group of friends to have children, what would she give to have a similarly sleep-deprived, worn-to-the-bone, exhausted rag of a shoulder to cry on, a friend who really really *gets* it, because she, as a fellow mother, is about to open her veins as well. Single women are sure that married women have no idea what it is *really* like to be this age and single, and married people are sure that single women have no idea what it is *really* like to be this age with children. And they're both right.

I always wanted five children. Don't ask. It has something to do with being the youngest of a family of four and wanting a younger sibling. Now, I'd sooner drink battery acid. But back in my innocence, I was awed, drunk with the notion that I could one day actually manufacture a real, live human being—every cell except one—from the lush tissue of my innards. I looked at pictures of women in agony as a human head appeared from between their hips and thought, I want to be her! I was a romantic. I knew that motherhood was in my future. I looked forward to it, anticipated it, yearned for it. And then, when my childbearing years came, in all their nubile glory, I did what every confused, extend-your-adolescence-through-your-late-thirties woman of my generation did. I ignored them. And while I was busy ignoring them, all my more mature I-can-accept-life-for-what-it-is-and-not-constantly-be-in-a-state-of-paralyzing-angst-about-what-it-isn't friends were having babies. Then one day I came to realize for the first time that there was a whole world of women out there that I could not relate to in the complete, truly cellular way I had before. I hated that. It was like they were all standing in a big circle comparing notes about stool color, teething remedies, and hours of labor and all I could do was to shout from across the room, "My sister said it was like shitting a watermelon!" Maybe they envied me for being able to eat a meal while it was still hot or pee in private, but it sure didn't feel that way to me. It's the greener grass thing. No matter how many hours I'd spent baby-sitting, no matter how many nieces and nephews I had, no matter how many friends I'd known who'd gone through it, I was like a virgin at an orgy. Well-meaning people who thought they were telling me something I didn't know always said the same things: "You'll never experience a love like this." "When it's yours, it is so different." Blah blah blah. What is it about people with children that makes them instant know-it-alls? This superior air always made me want to kick their teeth in, but I refrained, aware that such a gesture might be interpreted as overtly hostile, to say nothing of the high cost of dental work.

Usually, mothers didn't hold my barrenness against me; it was just that they were a part of something that I wasn't, and I'd never felt so separated from my female comrades. I wanted to rejoin the force. Be all that I could be. The toughest job I'd ever love. (As a mother now, of course, I look longingly at my friends without children and fantasize about stepping into their shoes for just a moment or two. An hour of unclaimed time? Hives of anticipation. An afternoon? Apoplectic. A whole day? Nothing short of orgasmic. We mothers are sorry heaps of human beings.) But, despite my deep desire, my wide breadth of knowledge on the subject, and my dazzling maturity, there was but one problem: no sperm—to say nothing of no money, no stability, no job, and no prospect for any of the above.

And even after a long, exhaustive search for the right man (see previous chapters), my problems *still* weren't solved. You would think, if you've gone out on more than one date in your life and have more than one brain cell, that the hardest part of this whole thing is finding a man with whom you have any real desire to spend the evening, let alone the rest of your life. I mean, after all, isn't that what the majority of your life has been focused on since the time you saw your first dreamboat playing Sky Masterson in the Camp Potowatomee production of *Guys and Dolls*? Of course it is. Honey, you have *suffered*. And finally, after a lifetime of toads and worms, you have picked the guy. The Guy! You have walked the walk, and finally it's a done deal. You are entitled to a nice, relaxing break from anxiety. You are ready to take your war-torn psyche into the backyard and ease it into a nice soft hammock, complete with a cool glass of lemonade, a mindless novel, and a warm spring breeze. This is the way you would like to stay for maybe a year or two, but then suddenly you have something totally new to worry about.

Conception.

The seemingly simple act of introducing a nice, menschedic sperm to a well-rounded, neither-whore-nor-madonna egg is not as simple as one might think (despite the fact that the luxurious egg has zillions of suitors every month, a much higher average than her long-suffering host body), at least not when you are some twenty years past your reproductive prime, or what gynecologists euphemistically call "AMA" (advanced maternal age).

This is when fantasies die hard. Really hard. Like the fantasy many women have of ceremonially throwing their birth control away at the altar of fertility while mumbling ancient chants, rubbing good-luck amulets, hopping on one foot

toward Mecca, and having the freest sex of their lives in order
to blend the essence of Man and Woman to create a brand
new miraculous being. The magical, mystical combination of
you and your loved one, growing cell by cell deep in the dark-
est folds of your body into a real-life honest-to-God person
who is one day going to experience things like rush hour,
heartbreak, service charges, and back fat.

"Wouldn't it be great," we used to sit around and say, "to
not have to worry about a slippery diaphragm that drips for
days, condoms that seem ridiculous in their low-tech function, or pills that fool your body into thinking that you're pregnant just to prevent you from getting that way?"

"Can you imagine," someone else would chime in dreamily,
"how much closer you would feel to your partner if you were
actually trying to *create* a baby, not avoid it? Think of the
romance! The excitement! The total abandonment! I can't
wait . . ." And the woman's voice would trail off, lost in the haze
of her image of an interlude that would defy tradition, expectation, and gravity. She was, in fact, picturing a scenario like this:

The lights are low. Candles are everywhere, their flames
dancing and flickering in the warm summer breeze that floats
through the open windows. The curtains (a white, translucent,
and sensuous sheer silk) billow suggestively in waves over the
windowsill. The door to the bedroom opens and a man who
looks remarkably like Harrison Ford (the perfect man because
he is both a Hollywood star *and* a carpenter) carries you, the
fantasizer, into the room, spinning you around playfully while
staring at you with a laserlike intensity that belies his aching
desire for you and locks you into his sights. He sets you down
gently on the moonlit bed as though you were a delicate gar-
land of hothouse flowers and, starting at the silky flaxen locks

that crown your head, he gently kisses you along every inch of your body, undressing you along the way as though unwrapping the most rare and delicate of antiquities. You, a bronze goddess whose sensuous curves transcend time and place, a woman who is soft, round, and ripe like the sweet juicy flesh of an exotic fig, reciprocate by exploring the maze of his body topography with your soft and agile tongue, leaving him in a moaning fervor, begging, pleading for more. Soon, you are stuck together, rolling around the sea of your bed like a dinghy lost in the storm of your passion. Time has stopped for the two of you as the world falls away and with it every care you had in the world. You enter another dimension completely, one you didn't even know existed, as you feel yourself melding into each other wholly and with sweet abandon. With a mighty crescendo, the earth opens and swallows you both as you fall into oblivion, two as one.

More likely, however, is a scenario something like this:

"Joe! the test line is darker than the sample line! We have to do it—*now!*"

"Now? The game is on."

"Yes, now. Now and for forty-eight hours from now."

"Then are we done for the month?"

"Yes. [*Under her breath*] Thank God."

"Okay, but could it wait till a commercial? The game's all tied up."

"Get your ass over here and pretend like I'm Michelle Pfeiffer, you sniveling excuse for a spermolater, I'm ovulating!"

"Okay, okay. Geez, it's like I'm just a piece of meat to you."

"I wish."

Then the lights go off, he does the things he always does, you do the things you always do, and about three and a half minutes later, it's over. You shove a few pillows under your hips in the hope of guiding the sperm to their final destination and put your legs up in the air to coax them to swim farther and faster. He catches his breath and then takes a big chance on his very life.

"Would you just blow a gasket if I went to watch the end of the game?"

And there you are, naked, legs akimbo, wondering whatever happened to the fantasies of yesteryear, thinking about starting a course for young women called "Reality 101," in which the opening lecture would include a good swift blow to the head with a lengthy piece of pipe.

I suppose there may be people who experience fantasy-like sex while trying to procreate, but I don't know any of them. Either that or they are (rightfully) too scared to tell me. Either way, I think the subject is best summed up by a friend of mine, mother of three, whose husband was in an amorous mood one day when she turned to him and said, "You have five fingers? *Use them!*" and continued to mop the kitchen floor.

And even when the trying-to-make-a-baby sex is successful and not fraught with unspoken expectations and disappointments, then comes the hardest part of all when you are anxious to get pregnant: the eternal, exhausting, obsessive waiting. Fourteen days before you can try to make a baby and fourteen days at least before you can rely on a home pregnancy test. Fourteen days! I mean, really, the world could be made from scratch twice over in that amount of time. It is torture of the highest magnitude. Torture that turns you into a lunatic, wondering, when you wake up bloated, if it is (possibly, hopefully, could it be?) an early sign of pregnancy or just the pan of brownies you ate last night in a fit of anxious pique. Is that breast tenderness the sign of a budding baby or just your monthly estrogen levels torturing you further? When you cry at an AT&T commercial, are you premenstrual or pre-baby? And then, toward the end of the month, when you can just stand it no longer, you feel compelled to start stocking up on pregnancy tests. And even though you can't expect accurate results until at least day 28, on day 25 you start peeing into a cup because you just have to do something to make yourself feel less helpless, even to the tune of fifteen bucks a pee.

And every month that that thin pink line eludes you, you sink deeper and deeper into a kind of letdown hangover, wondering why you didn't have children when you were in your early twenties, despite the fact that you would be divorced, broke, and mentally unstable had you gone that route (who cares, you say to yourself, as long as you were kicking out healthy eggs on a regular basis). And then, when days 28, 29, 30, 31, 32, and 33 go by with no pink line in sight, you think to yourself, sure it's most likely that I'm about to get my period but maybe, just maybe, I didn't ovulate until day 19 and the three-day-old sperm were able to limp along to that egg— since I was standing on my head the whole time—and, in a final gasp of strength, break into the egg's barrier, creating a brand-new life, and the hormones just haven't had the time to build up enough steam to show up on the pregnancy test. Didn't I just hear about a friend's sister-in-law's best friend whose cousin was actually pregnant but it didn't show up on the 99.9 percent accurate home test? That could be me! And then five minutes later, just when you have become absolutely sure that you are indeed pregnant, planning out just how you'll tell everyone, what you'll name the little darling, and what color to paint the nursery, you get your period and end up bawling your eyes out on the floor of the bathroom, feeling barren, hopeless, and like you never want to have sex again.

And then the whole thing begins again, and you are left with nothing but cramps, stained underwear (the little brown shmutz theory proves correct yet again), and another fourteen or so days before you even start with the ovulation predictor kits, let alone the monthly ritual of sex-on-demand, which can turn the most erotic couple's fantastic love life into something with all the excitement of soil chemistry. And in your more cogent moments, you want to go back to being the misty-eyed girl who dreamed of pitching her diaphragm over a cliff, thereby starting the most romantic, erotic, and titillating episodes of her life, and grab her by the neck and shout, "What the hell is the matter with you, you delusional yutz! This is one of the things that breaks couples up right and left, that ends in blame, shame, and misery! Wake up and smell that coffee of disillusionment, babe! Get with reality!" The misty-eyed girl of your youth, of course, goes sniveling off into a corner in minor hysteria at the bleak future you have just doomed her to. But you feel a little better, so what do you care? If you're gonna suffer, you want everyone to suffer. If your fantasies don't come true, no one's should, and in my opinion, honey, that's only fair. And this is only day 1 of your cycle. She should be glad she didn't catch you on day 27.

Of course, by the time I actually got off my ass (or, if I want to be anatomically accurate, got on it) and started trying (always a big euphemism—and easier than saying yeah, we threw away the birth control a year ago, are having sex according to a temperature chart, are subtly holding each other in contempt in light of our collective failure, and are spending a lot of time in long, silent pauses that are about the only pregnant things around, goddammit), I found out that ovulation just wasn't something my body loved to do. Maybe once in a while, but every month, what're you, kidding? I am lazy down to my ovaries. So I joined the millions of women who take little pills to give an ovum the incentive it needs to break free and take a merry trip down the fallopian tube in the hope of meeting the sperm of her dreams.

Paul and I went on vacation. I caught a whopping head cold. Whopping. With fever. We tried anyway (always a treat when your head feels like a wrecking ball, you can't breathe, and you can't take any drugs on the off-off chance that you could be two hours pregnant). When it didn't work I went back to the doctor so she could make sure the drugs weren't causing any blistering cysts on my ovaries before giving me the next month's supply. She looked at my temperature chart and said, "So why are you so sure you're not pregnant?"

"I'm certain I'm getting my period. I can tell. I'm never on time. My breasts are killing me and I already started spotting. Plus, if you must know, I've also taken four pregnancy tests in the last three days. So, more drugs?"

"We're going to do a test anyway. Did you give us a urine specimen?"

"Yeah, yeah, yeah." Fine with me, I thought. I had taken maybe eight pregnancy tests at her office prior to various tests, so one more was nothing. She opened the door a crack.

"Do an HcG on her, will you?" she said to the nurse. Thirty seconds later, the nurse walked in with a big smile on her face, holding a big pink plus sign at eye level so all could see. I went totally blank for a second. I was utterly stunned.

"Are you sure that was *my* urine? Gwen? Macsai?" I had to ask. There are just so many Dixie cups full of pee at a gynecol-

ogist's office, one can't be too sure. The nurse nodded. "Oh
my God! I can't believe it!" I said as I hugged the doctor, the
nurse, and the blood-pressure stand.

"But wait!" I blurted out. "What about the fever I had? The
spotting? And what about the diet Coke I just drank?"

"You're fine," the doc reassured me, and sent me on my
way. I went directly to the drugstore to buy a few more pregnancy tests. What did they know? I'm a hands-on kind of person, I had to see for myself. The pink line was ever so faint.
So I tried it again the next morning. It was still faint, but
there. How could that be? I felt the exact same way I had the
day before and the day before.

I wanted a sign. Something more than a due date so far off
that calendars for that year weren't even in print yet. I wanted
to *feel* it, to know, to have a shred of physical proof that the
greatest biological feat of all time was already well under way
somewhere under my skin and between my bones. After all,
until your first fifty-yard dash to the bathroom, the whole
thing is just so conceptual, if you know what I mean. I walked
around the streets feeling like I alone knew a great secret and
didn't have to tell one living soul until I wanted to. Oh, that
was a great feeling. I was finally standing at the sanctified
threshold of motherhood, the very brink of life itself. I'd pictured myself there a thousand times, and now there I was,
with no idea what I was actually *doing* there. Me. Not her or
her or her or her, me. How very strange.

As it happened, Paul was out of town the day of my doctor's appointment, away from a phone all day, due to return
that evening. I had scheduled my annual self-pitying massage
with a friend that evening and Paul was going to meet me in
the bar of the hotel in which I had the massage. My friend had

to cancel, so I went alone, examining myself closely in one of the many full-length locker-room mirrors. No different. Not a mole had moved. Nothing. I weighed myself a few times on each scale, waiting for the masseuse. I told her my secret.

"Then I will avoid your entire midsection, since I know someone who miscarried after a vigorous massage."

Not exactly a confidence builder. But not to worry, since I have rarely met a masseuse who meets my desire to be worked over like an outlaw (the sandbag-breasted, eucalyptus-leaf-toting, gargantuan nude excepted). I could've felt better with a $1.95 backscrather from Walgreen's. After putting up with her pansy hands for an hour, I showered and looked in the mirror again (no change) and dressed. I went to the bar and ordered herbal tea. I was prepared when Paul arrived. I presented him with the positive pregnancy test with the big pink plus on it (the doctor's test, which she gave me as a souvenir), nicely gift wrapped. He opened it and looked at me quizzically.

"What is this?"

"You don't know?"

"Am I supposed to?"

"Yes!" I bellowed, and patted myself on the back for having anticipated this very reaction. I pulled out Plan B: another gift, this one a copy of Dave Barry's *Babies and Other Hazards of Sex*. I gave it to him. He opened it and stared at me blankly. Then, as though someone had just dropped a piano on his head, he got it.

"You're kidding!"

"No sir, Big Daddy!"

We did a little jig, exchanged high fives, hugged, kissed, and went to our friends' house to drink sparkling cider.

Still, as the days and weeks passed, I wanted proof. Something I could hear, touch, smell, taste, or see, besides the inside of the toilet bowl. Those weeks crawled by slowly, and one day the nurse came at me with something akin to a Geiger counter, greased me up, and started listening to the abdominal concerts provided by mysterious body churnings below my belly button. And while she moved the gelled-up sensor around like it was a little ice skater doing figure eights on my belly, she suddenly stopped when we heard a rhythmic swishing like a really moist radar signal from a 1960 submarine movie.

"There it is!" she smiled, "Your baby's heartbeat!"

A heartbeat? Already? Just ten weeks prior, they were two cells having a quiet romantic dinner, sizing each other up over dessert.

THE EGG: "I just love a sperm with a sense of humor!"
THE SPERM: "Did I ever mention that I have a black belt in addition to my Olympic Gold in the ten-centimeter backstroke?"

And now, suddenly, they are a brand-new heart, beating wildly, pumping energy into the machinery that is working day and night to get this thing ready for delivery on time. It's all so beautifully . . . relentless.

Things medical fascinate me beyond reason. I would have gone to medical school if I hadn't had to take any math or chemistry. But I didn't, so I just like to pretend I did. And when it is something happy you are investigating, like pregnancy, and it is already under way, why, the bookshelf is just overflowing with things to tell you. Much of this information I had already read while anticipating this day (at the age of sixteen, huddled in the bathroom with my copy of *Our Bodies, Ourselves*), but not all. I started reading everything I could to try to anticipate any symptoms that might be coming my way. I always like to be prepared. Upon seeing the vast number of books on the subject, however, I blanched. These were some of the things the books told me that I might have to look forward to:

Fatigue
Depression
Frequent urination
Nausea
Vomiting
Excessive salivation
Heartburn
Indigestion
Flatulence
More flatulence
Bloating
Food aversions
Aversions to smells
Cravings
Painful breasts
Enlarged breasts
Darkening of the aureole
PMS-like symptoms, including
   weepiness, mood swings,
   irritability, irrationality
Overwhelming fear about the
   health of the baby
Constipation
Occasional headaches
Migraines

Occasional faintness or
   dizziness
Blue vein lines under the skin
   of your breasts
Spider veins on legs
Acne
Trouble sleeping
Stretch marks
Reduced sexual drive
Increased sexual drive
Abdominal cramps after
   orgasm
Increased pulse rate
Increase in body temperature
   for nine months
Bleeding gums
Increase in appetite
Slowed digestion
Swelling of ankles and feet
Varicose veins
Hemorrhoids
Whitish vaginal discharge
Increased lubrication during
   sex
Breathlessness

Forgetfulness

Nasal congestion

Snoring

Gestational diabetes

Lower abdominal achiness

Leg cramps

Backache

Easier or more difficult orgasms

Skin pigmentation changes on
    abdomen and face

Fast-growing hair and nails

Swelling of feet

Itchy abdomen

Tingling sensation like pins and
    needles in extremities

Toxemia or preeclampsia

Leaky breasts

Incontinence

Buttock and pelvis discomfort
    and achiness

Development of a slight heart
    murmur

Change in eyesight

Change in equilibrium

And that list is by no means complete. For they don't mention some of the more graphic details, like the new body topography of lumps, bumps, and dark raisinlike moles that mysteriously appear on your already freckled skin. Like the feeling that your vagina is so weighed down it feels like it is going to slowly ooze its way out of your body. Like even *more* facial hair. Like the fact that you may have to give your crotch a crew cut to avoid a lot of nasty tangling and clumps of dried you-goo. Then there are the yeast infections, a particularly evil twist on an already unwieldy situation. I myself had never suffered one of these nasty beasts until late in my first pregnancy, when I felt like I wanted to claw at my crotch like a dog pawing for a bone. The doctor gave me medicine and in all seriousness told me to go home and blow-dry my pubic hair to keep the area dry. Maybe, I thought to myself, I should consider a whole new style while I'm at it. A part down the center? A dye job? Maybe extensions. I promptly went out and bought a sixteen-dollar blow-dryer (most women—and my father—already have such appliances at home in their medicine cabinets or linen closets, but I have a particular aversion to these devices. I would rather have my hair freeze into icicles on my head—which it does every winter—than stand there blowing hot air at myself every morning). However, the awkward stance of a very pregnant woman, already toppling from one side to another just to ambulate, trying to maneuver a blow-dryer between her legs, proved to be too much for even me, and the blow-dryer was added to the junk heap of unused appliances. I just gritted my teeth and toweled more vigorously.

As it happens, however, I wouldn't have needed a book to tell me about all of these symptoms of pregnancy. Following an irresistible, seemingly primitive urge, women everywhere see your swelling belly and tell you the very worst thing about their pregnancy and delivery, whether you like it or not.

"My nipples were inverted and all my hair fell out," one woman told me cheerfully.

"Even with the episiotomy, I was ripped to shreds," said another with a big smile. "And the irony of the whole thing is, as bad as I ripped, I didn't even *feel* it because the pain of the baby coming out was so great!"

"I pushed so hard I burst a blood vessel in my eye, but that was no big deal."

And then the topper: "You'll be fine. Most women are . . . except my sister-in-law, of course, who was paralyzed by her epidural."

One of my favorites came from my sister when she was asking me how I felt later in the pregnancy. I told her that I felt like my crotch was a swollen mass of weary flesh, and that all of the blood in my body had traveled to that one bloated site. She laughed and told me that a friend of hers was so engorged late in her pregnancy, she could bring herself to orgasm simply by walking down the street.

Okay, so maybe this pregnancy wasn't such a big, sentimental, romantic thing after all (even though I was the only one in my childbirth class who actually cried all the way through the birthing film). I mean, let's face it. You think you are caught up in doing something wondrous and magnificent comparable only to the divine creation of the sun, the stars, and the sea. You want to be at one with the growing organism inside of you, but in the harsh reality of the morning light, it turns out you're nothing but a host. A host! A powerless shell. You are a harbor, a vessel, a mother ship. This little blastocyte has a life of its own, literally. It has you wrapped around its budding little finger, completely at its mercy. And by now, it is having its way with you. Who knew that an organism the size of a lima bean could be such a tyrant, making you crave food and then move it away with disgust after one bite, filling you with a need to sleep that is so pervasive, only a narcoleptic could sympathize, and making you so spacey that when you sneeze, you bless yourself. And then finally, after making your husband get rid of the coffee grinder, his shampoo, his toothpaste, and all strong cheese in the refrigerator, the months start to creep by and suddenly, out of nowhere, your stomach starts resembling a nice, soft pitcher's mound.

Now, personally, let me just say that my stomach has *always* been—let me think of how to put this—a protruding one. You know, the kind that has to be set free after a big meal. I wouldn't say that I am obsessed with the soft, round, fleshy nature of my midsection, even though it is the first thing I take stock of in the morning and the last thing I size up at night. And I'm not proud that the actual quality of my day is often directly proportional to that very protrusion. Big gut, bad day; little gut, good day. But after a lifetime of trying to hide my abdominal rotundity under elastic waistbands and vertical stripes, I finally found the perfect solution to my problem.

Pregnancy. And the single best thing about it?

Never having to hold your stomach in!

It's amazing, a liberation like no other. The ultimate freedom. The very zenith of relaxation. Your stomach is finally free to roam at will. To protrude with pride. To roll and expand like ocean swells. No more snaps, buttons, buckles, belts, zippers, darts, or hooks. It's any girl's wet dream. Eat all you want, bust a gut, no one will notice 'cause you are as big as a house anyway and your pants have long been abandoned for a burlap sack disguised as a maternity jumper.

Soon, you weigh more than your husband—and all your old boyfriends combined. The baby within is doing its best Esther Williams, making you feel like a human aquarium, which is exactly what you are. The queen Sea Monkey. You are a victim of your body's physics, to say nothing of its hormones, now reaching record levels. Muzak makes you misty eyed. You cry at the nightly news jingle. Ken Barlow (Kenny to me), the Minneapolis weatherman, reduced me to tears every night in a commercial where he was shown sledding with his children in the snow. My back hurt, my muscles ached, I couldn't bend down to tie my own shoes or pick up my own leg to shave it. Then my innie turned into an outie.

I was forced to rethink things.

I stopped thinking of pregnancy as the miracle of life. Miracle shmiracle! I started to think of it as the only time in my life when my stomach would truly be hard. Comments like, "Should you really be *eating* that?" "Wow, is there any chance you could be having twins?" and "You know, your breasts really are *enormous*!" These are just things that the pregnant woman, as human receptacle, has to put up with, since everyone who is not pregnant sees a swelling belly as license to wax freely about your size, shape, weight gain, and coming torture in the delivery room. One friend of mine ran out of patience for just such comments by her ninth month, which sort of goes without saying. She was, by all measurements, huge. And she was out at a coffee cart before work one morning when a man stopped and smiled at her lovingly. "God bless!" he said to her in a warm tone. She stared back at him. "Fuck you!" she yelled, at which point the man turned away, horrified. Maybe he learned his lesson about the disposition of a woman in her ninth month of pregnancy happening upon a well-meaning stranger: starving piranha meets juicy fillet.

OH, BABY

I realize why women die in childbirth—it's preferable.
—SHERRY GLASER

YOU CANNOT CARRY A baby around in your belly for nine months and not become a little curious or perhaps mildly obsessed with the question, Who is this person? What will s/he be like, and what will s/he look like? I'd seen that my sisters' kids were cute and my brother's boys were handsome, but just what kind of little face my little shmoody would have was a mystery too confounding. And then, as I found myself spacing out during the sermon at one more set of high-holiday services, it suddenly dawned on me. It came to me like a vision, and then all of a sudden, I *knew* what my baby would look like.

Shecky Green.

Or Buddy Hackett. Or, at best, maybe Uncle Fester. I just figured it was my genetic destiny to bear a child that closely resembled a borscht-belt comic. Dark, hairy, and all scrunched up.

Then, on New Year's Day, I woke up feeling crampy. The cramps came in waves. They were two and a half minutes apart. Paul was timing them on a Michael Jordon stopwatch he had bought two months previously and had tested out every hour or so since then. I turned to him.

"Do you think I should call the midwife?"

"Of course you should."

"I don't want to bother her."

He rolled his eyes and gave me the phone. "Call." I dialed the number that was written as big as graffiti next to every phone.

"I'm in labor!" I said with excitement.

"Really? Great. Call back when you are in pain."

This is not a direct quote, since nurse midwives are my favorite people on the planet, but essentially, that is what she said. I was crestfallen. I thought, can't I come now?

"Take a bath," she suggested, "and call me back as things progress." Paul went up to run a bath and came down with a long face.

"I can't believe it. The drain is backing up. There is crud and shit all over the tub. It's disgusting. Don't go up there," he said.

"Are you kidding me? Jesus," I said. I felt that my bathtub had it in for me. I tried to think about whose bathtub I could confiscate for a while. But it was Christmastime and everyone was out of town. Then it hit me. My friend, the sainted Mary Ellen, was still in town. We drove across town to her house, where I walked directly to the bathroom, stripped, and waded into the tub. Her daughter Maeve kept walking in, saying, "Mommy, why is she in our bathtub? Are you staying here? *My* mommy takes showers." The sainted Mary Ellen ran interference for me. "Gwen is going to have a baby. Look at her big belly. Look at the grimace on her face. See? Now come into the kitchen with me, please." Paul was sitting on the floor of the bathroom keeping his hand on the stopwatch, scrawling the contraction start and stop times on a soggy piece of paper like he was taking down the Ten Comandments. After a half hour or forty minutes, I couldn't take it anymore. I was starting to understand what they meant when they told me not to come in until I couldn't walk or talk through the contractions. Paul had to hoist me out of the tub. I was like a slippery sumo wrestler. I threw my clothes on, growled at Mary Ellen's husband, who had just come in the house with a big, friendly "Hi!" and went down to the kitchen to call the midwife back.

"Let me hear you through one contraction."

I thought this was a little on the sadistic side, but I obliged. We idiotically talked about the weather (bad), how long it would take to get there (fifteen minutes), and other assorted details for ninety seconds. Then a contraction hit. I moaned loudly and involuntarily. She was impressed, saying, "Now we're getting someplace, come on in." Apparently, you have to be all but muttering the Lord's Prayer before they want to have anything to do with you. I got to the hospital, got into another bathtub, and labored there for a while before a nurse got me out to check my dilation in centimeters.

"That's great! You're a generous three."

I stared at her. "Three? That's it? You've got to be kidding!?"

"Okay, three and a half. Some people labor for hours just to get to one."

Well, screw them, I thought. We're talking about *me*.

"You're doing great," she said with a smile, and left. Janet, the labor-and-delivery nurse, was there to pick up the pieces and help me back into the tub. Paul was sitting right next to the tub with the trusty stopwatch. With every contraction, I gripped the handicapped rail with my left hand and the collar of Paul's sweater with my right. Every once in a while I would hear him gasp for air, pointing to his neck in an effort to urge me to loosen my grip so that he might live to see his child. It's not that I was trying to strangle him, it's just that at that angle, with that girth, a laboring woman in a tub doesn't have a lot of wiggle room, and his collar was the perfect height to offer the resistance I felt I had to have. Or at least that's what I told him.

When I got to five centimeters, I yanked the midwife over by the arm, stared her down, and said "If I *did* want something for pain, what are my choices?"

"We can give you a shot of Nubane. It'll take the edge off."

I stuck out my biggest vein.

Then I went from five to ten centimeters in an hour. Nothing could take the edge off of that. If you've ever had *intense* gastric pain or maybe passed a mirror ball, then you know what I mean. I lived that hour in thirty-second increments. Thirty seconds till the contraction would end. Thirty more of glorious, sea-parting relief. Thirty more of mentally prepping for the next contraction. Thirty more for the contraction to build to its full electroshock height. Thirty more of full throttle, thousand-volt, white-knuckle, strangle-Paul pain, and then biblical relief once again. After an hour of this, I felt something pop. My water broke. I looked up at Janet. Something's different, I told her, *really* different. I felt like I was really starting to lose control. The midwife came in, checked me, and urged me to get up on the bed while she put on her gown and a new pair of gloves. Ten minutes and two gargantuan, devil-pulling-your-pelvis-apart-like-a-Thanksgiving-wishbone pushes later, my daughter slithered out and took her first breath.

Surprisingly, she looked nothing like Shecky Green. Or Buddy Hackett. Not even a trace of Uncle Fester. A little girl who was pink and creamy, like an alabaster cherub. Blue eyes, fair skin, and a strawberry tint to her peachy little head.

I thought I had a Protestant child.

Who knew? My mother, who was on the next plane to Minnesota, had only six words to say on the subject: "She doesn't have a Macsai nose!" And when my father followed her a day later, he literally, I swear to God, took one look at the baby and said, verbatim, "She doesn't have a Macsai nose!" which tells you less about their paranoia and more about the overwhelmingly consistent characteristic that has been passed down from generation to generation in my family. Of course, at that very moment, somewhere in Connecticut, a couple was looking down into their bassinet wondering, "Honey, does she look *swarthy* to you? She looks *swarthy* to me."

Having a baby was as close to a religious experience as I'll ever get. There she was, a glorious person from whom light itself seemed to emanate. While my brain was swept into overdrive with thoughts of grandeur—"Oh my God, she is so beautiful," "Life is so profound"—I couldn't help but also ponder, "I wonder how much weight I just lost?"

Meanwhile, everyone else could apparently think of only one thing: *"So, what's her name?"*

Her *name*. As though it would actually be possible to think of one word worthy enough. At six pounds, thirteen ounces— at any weight—she was gigantic, enormous, expansive beyond measure—and this gargantuan person, who was millions and millions of years in the making, who came to me full of the possibilities of all the universe, I had to define in a syllable or two? Impossible.

Then it came to me: Ruby.

I spent all of my days with Ruby smelling her forehead. In the morning I was so glad to see her, I forgot that sleep deprivation is a form of torture in many countries. In the afternoon when I rocked her to sleep, I felt that the world began and ended right here in that room, and in the evenings when we danced around the living room I had to use every ounce of self-restraint to keep from licking her all over.

As prepared as you can be, you can never be really prepared. Who knew, for instance, that overnight you could go from a 36B to a 38F? (One has to wonder, do they even make a "G"?) In my former life, a breast was just, you know, a breast. Now, my breasts alone would have required two carry-ons (if they were detachable, they would *be* two carry-ons). I was a living geyser, likely to blow at any moment. And who knew that stretch marks were purple? Who knew that you'd be called upon to feed the baby on one breast and express milk out of the other, all while opening the mail, eating lunch, writing thank-you notes, and talking on the phone. But if you happen to have mastered the art of picking things up with your toes, you're already way ahead of the game.

In fact, all parts of the body come into play for a new mother. Aside from the fact that you are either leaking or bleeding or sweating from every hole and pore, each body part is like a well-oiled component of you; you are a human Swiss Army knife, capable of everything from taking out a splinter while trimming your nails to sawing through a small branch while opening a bottle of wine. Your elbow, for instance, is no longer the joint between your shoulder and wrist; it is a door stopper, a card sorter, and, if you are agile enough, a tool for typing while both hands are occupied. You are a human napkin, a twenty-four-hour janitor without the benefit of sawdust to clean up the puke.

Even the face comes in handy (no pun intended). For the first time, I was glad that my nose is the size it is. It gave my daughter something to chew on. In fact, my whole body became a topographical curiosity, a maze of lumps and bumps there for her rubbing, pinching, slapping, sucking, tweaking, and petting pleasure—and, I might add, the feeling of having a baby in your arms, licking and kissing and biting and burrowing, is quite possibly the most sensuous experience I've ever known. You just want to eat every inch of her beautiful, creamy self.

The touch of baby skin is the elixir that fixes all ills. And like freshly risen bread dough, a baby's belly demands to be consuuuuumed. When she looks at me, she doesn't just gaze at me, she *pours* herself into me. When I carry her, she combs my hair with her delicate little fingers (just prior to ripping it from my scalp), and when I nurse her she caresses my breast as though it were sacred. When I walk into the room, she bounces so hard and smiles so wide she looks as though she's about to blast off. It's love in its most perfect state, and there is nothing rarer than that.

You see, adults are so complicated that love between them is necessarily and inherently flawed (see every other chapter of this book). The much-sought-after all-consuming, picture-perfect love worthy of a movie of the week is virtually nonexistent, unless of course it's unrequited or you are under twelve. So we spend a lifetime searching for perfection (you are everything I've ever wanted . . . I love you more than life itself . . .) only to have reality rear its ugly head every time (did I mention that I've never really been attracted to you, thought I could overcome it, but can't?).

But then a baby is born and explains everything that ever was, is, and will be. Boom! There it is, the love you've always dreamed of, safely swaddled and staring at you, so stinging in its purity, all you can do is cry your eyes out. Although some of that may be sleep deprivation—a state that puts you constantly on the precipice of insanity and will make you weep uncontrollably at the slightest provocation, like say, a red light, or—even worse—Raffi.

Extended sleep deprivation feels like someone opened up a tap at the bottom of your feet and drained all the blood out of your body, replacing it with lead. You wake up every day feeling crusty, like you've been breaded and fried. The exhaustion follows you around all day—as you try to coax her to sleep by driving her around the entire state holding a bottle with your right hand, shifting with your left, steering with your knees, and heading in any direction that puts her side of the car in the shade. In the bleary hours of the morning, it haunts you like your own personal cloud as you stand over your crying baby's crib at 3 A.M. You go to reach for her only to find yourself utterly paralyzed, and hearing voices—mostly of female relatives.

"Let her cry it out, or she'll be clingy and dependent!"

"Pick her up, or she'll be scarred for life!"

But the worst part of sleep deprivation is when you *finally* get a few golden moments to yourself to catch up on your sleep and you lay your deliriously weary head on your pillow, and just as you are drifting off to blissful slumber, you are suddenly ambushed by horrible, grotesque, *morbid thoughts.* Vivid scenes of all the terrible things that could happen to your little sugarplum come at you like thunderbolts, zapping your brain and sending it soaring right out of your skull, into the depraved pits of despair. Choking, car accidents, disease, deranged strangers, freak accidents, and pestilence consume your every thought. And you think to yourself, I'll just keep her here in the house for the next forty years or so, and she'll be *fine.* (But then you start thinking, What if I am nibbling her little fingers at the very moment that there is an earthquake and I end up biting off my own daughter's digits?)

Motherhood is far and away the single hardest thing I've ever done. And yet, all I wanted to do was do it again. And again after that. I found myself staring at pregnant women, jealous of their beautiful, ripe, perfectly rounded bellies. I wanted another, and another, and maybe a few more after that. And there were only three things stopping me, other than my bank account: my husband, who oddly enough thinks two or three is plenty; my age, which was advancing at a rate I never thought possible; and the pressing feeling that to have another is to cheat on my first. To be grossly unfaithful in the greatest of all love affairs. I felt like an adulteress, an ingrate, Benedict Arnold. How could I let another being encroach on our beautiful little love bubble? How could I cause my baby a moment's distress? I knew that I would try to give her siblings, but what if she is one of these children who wants to throw their sister in the garbage can or return her from whence she came?

When she's twenty-three and I'm paying for her therapy, I can just tell that *this* is where it'll all start. There she'll be, on the couch, staring at the ceiling, saying, "My earliest memory? The birth of my baby brother. And if I can be frank, I think that all my deep-rooted feelings of abandonment and betrayal can be traced back to that very moment."

I couldn't bear the thought of breaking the spell between us, even though she'll get over it, I'll get over it, blah blah blah. I felt guilty and unsure. I mean, what if the next one turns out to be another Squeaky Fromme? Or worse yet, Marla Maples? I couldn't bear toting around a child who insisted on matching shoes and bag. But that's the beauty of it, the mystery, the great unknown and all that. Only one sperm out of millions gets its way. If the guy to his left got there first, you could end up with Boris Karloff instead of Karla Bonoff, Pee-wee Herman instead of Pee Wee Reese. And instead of Yo-Yo Ma, just a plain yo-yo.

So, I just figured, Hey, I didn't wait until my ovaries were starting to calcify to start this whole baby thing for nothing. I am now mature and wise and completely unflappable, so when sibling rivalry is at its worst and they hate each other as toddlers and fight like cats and dogs as adolescents, I'll just wait patiently until they come to love and cherish each other as adults. Then I can sit back and reap the rewards of the seeds I've sown. I'll be settled and secure. Wise and weathered. Of course, by the time this actually happens, it's also quite likely that I will be, honestly speaking, dead as a doornail.

In the meantime, Ruby was a little kumquat, Sugar Pop, Tootsie Roll, and bubelah extraordinaire. I couldn't even fathom what she would look like or act like in a year or ten. I think the only thing I can bet on is that over the next twenty years, she's bound to despise me for at least five of them.

Then, as time went by, I started to obsess over the next one. What would *another* child of mine be like, who would that person be? I had to know. I wanted to have another one before Ruby was too old to feel dethroned. And so, despite my guilt about ruining Ruby's life, I figured she'd be grateful for a sibling, even if it was only to post bail every now and then. And that's how, fifteen months later, I found myself knocked up yet again.

BRINGING UP BABY

I want to have children while my parents are
still young enough to take care of them.

—RITA RUDNER

BECOMING A PARENT IS

a complicated business. It can upset the applecart you formerly knew as your life in any one of thousands of ways.
Some you're prepared for, some you aren't. And the ones that
catch you by surprise, those are the funkiest. They're also the
ones that no one tells you about, which is why I am here.

Parenting styles, for instance. Even though all parents
are feeling their way blind through the child-rearing jungle
that has become their existence, they are all convinced that
their way of blind feeling is the right way. The mothers who
won't allow ketchup bottles on the dinner table (it should be
poured into a glass bowl and served with a spoon) versus the
ones who make mud pies on the new carpet and think nothing of it. The ones who cure their own hams versus the ones
who have a bench dedicated to them at McDonald's. You
know what I mean. Who knew that these kinds of things can
cause old friends to look down their noses at one another
and perfect strangers to become best friends? I mean, when
you are a young girl, there is nothing that can separate you

from your best friends. Nothing. You are as inseparable as H_2 and O.

When you are an adolescent, a few things can separate you from your best friends. Dating your best friend's boyfriend will do it, as will dating your best friend's ex-boyfriends, so that might be something to stay away from. Even dating your best friend's crush-person gets dicey. Also, there is sometimes a natural parting of ways when the upbringing and temperament of one friend may lead her toward Junior Achievement while the other dives headlong into tongue piercing. This may ripple the waters of a childhood bond.

But as a parent, child rearing is the thing that can cause the biggest rift. If you had a hidden microphone on the table at any coffee shop where mothers gather to chew the fat, this is the kind of thing you would hear:

"Did you see the way Emily has her mother wrapped around her finger? Haven't they ever heard of setting *limits*? They are just begging for trouble down the road. I swear to God, if she were my child, I would be all over her. She is just wild!"

"Well, I don't know which is better, that or the way Josie just hovers over little Sammy. She won't go visiting if someone has so much as a runny nose. She watches him like a hawk and practically chews his food for him. Now there's a kid who is going to rebel big time."

"Did you know that baby Hershel still has a pacifier? And he still wakes up four times a night? I don't know how his parents can stand it."

"How about Zoe? That child has more toys than God. And do you see how they dress that poor child? Its like she's running for Miss Toddler USA. It's sick."

"At least those parents have time to dress her. Did you know that Judy just took a job as a vice president? I don't know why they had kids in the first place. I don't think they see their kids more than five hours a week. No wonder they spoil them rotten. Guilt city."

"All I can say is that I'm glad you all are perfect, just like me. What a relief."

This conversation happens on every park bench, every swimming pool edge, at every zoo and every amusement park. Wherever mothers gather, mothers judge. And not without reason (speaking as a mother). Nothing is worse than when a good friend or relative is raising her children completely differently than you think she should or than you would raise yours.

Let's say you are over at a friend's house, a friend who has a spirited four-year-old who is screaming and yelling and throwing tantrum after tantrum while the parents sit quietly and say sotto voce, "Priscilla dear, you know the rules in this house, we don't throw things through the window, dear. Please stop, sweetie. Okay, please put down Mommy's Fabergé egg, my little pumpkin. I think we need to have a talk about mutual respect of each other's belongings. Now now, we don't want any more crayons on the newly painted walls, darling, so let's work together here. That shoe doesn't belong in the blender." Meanwhile you are sitting on your hands to stop from wringing the young Priscilla's little neck.

This is one of parenthood's biggest shockers: thinking that your children will bind you closer to your cherished friends, until you wake up one day to find that you have replaced them with total strangers who happen to be parents of your *children's* friends. This is because you cannot watch as people you once knew and loved are wildly indulging their children;

putting up with husbands who expect the house to be clean and the kids to be in their jammies with their teeth brushed before you can have a cup of coffee with a girlfriend; or parents who try to control everything in the children's lives and are up nights if the kids aren't potty trained by eighteen months. Unlike some of the other idiosyncrasies you have noticed in your friends over the years, the things that you dismiss as "just a part of them" that never really bothered you, different child-rearing styles are not something you can let just roll off your back. So you either have a frank discussion about how you disagree with what they are doing or how they disagree with what you are doing (never happens), or you drift slowly away (always happens).

There is, however, one mitigating factor in this whole process, one thing that strikes fear into the heart of the most confident parent. And that is when you see a child who is going through a really rotten phase, a phase when you want to hang him by his thumbnails: whining constantly, screaming and yelling all the time, kicking, throwing things, biting, or plotting a mutiny. You walk away shaking your head, thinking, "My kid will never be like *that!*" And then one day, six months later, you wake up to find that your adorable boo-boo has been kidnapped and replaced with a facsimile who is whining constantly, screaming and yelling all the time, kicking, throwing things, biting, and plotting a mutiny. It's like when you are in your early twenties and you look at your parents' marriage and you think, I will never have a marriage like *that!* only to wake up fifteen years later thinking, "We sound just like my parents!" Which just goes to show you that you can't judge other people till you've walked a mile in their shoes, as Atticus Finch so beautifully said. (Is Gregory Peck the most handsome man alive, by the way, or what?) And mothers who walk away saying, "My kids will never be like *that!*" have to pause for an addendum that reads, "I sure as hell hope to God."

But, as it is the right of all unmarried persons to believe that they and they alone will be able to break the chain and finally get this marriage thing right (after all, how hard can it be?), so it is the right of all parents to believe that they and they alone hold the secret to raising the perfect child—after all, just look at their shining examples. As my mother once said, "Babies are babies and temperaments are temperaments. The people who have an easy baby the first time around righteously think they did everything right, and then, when their next kid is a pain in the neck, they toss it up to temperament so it doesn't reflect badly on them. Either way, the one thing you can be sure of is that everyone blames the mother."

Parents go wild over certain things. Like swearing, one of my very favorite subjects. I think it is hilarious, since I happen to come from a particularly foul-mouthed family. Mouths like truck drivers, some would say, to which I say, what is wrong with a truck driver's mouth? Is it any better or worse than the mouth of a librarian, Las Vegas showgirl, Tibetan monk, or presidential appointee? No. In fact, I think that deep in his heart of hearts, a presidential appointee would love to be able to stand up in his confirmation hearing, look the distinguished members of Congress in the eye, and tell them all to go to hell, goddammit. It just isn't done, so they don't do it. But since we non–presidential appointees don't have such societal girdles restricting us, we are free to speak our minds, and if our minds are filled with swear words, like mine happens to be, so be it. Some people's brains think in pictures, some in concepts, and some in words. Mine is clearly the latter. I can't help it if they all contain four letters.

I love swearing. It's most fulfilling. Swear words are full of consonants that your tongue can slap around your mouth and spit out like so many wads of tobacco juice with no disgusting residual effects, other than offending people. And since I am not easily offended, I am of the firm belief that other people shouldn't be either. Why should they get their shorts in a knot over whether you have a foul mouth? My attitude is clearly a result of my upbringing in a house where my father, a little Hungarian, mastered the art of the English expletive before he learned the past tense. My mother, I should say, also gets particular pleasure out of hurling a few curse words out into the cosmos when she is on a tear about one thing or another. It all seems pretty harmless to me. Some may pale, but it makes me feel right at home. Nobody blanches at my house when you express yourself crudely. Men I've dated have been shocked by my father's relaxed use of the seamier sides of the language, but as soon as we would leave the house, they never said to me, "God, your family is trash!" They always looked considerably more relaxed as they bounded down the stairs, saying, "Your parents are so *cool*!" I'm telling you, everyone wants to be a swearer, some people are just more repressed than others.

But this seems to become a particular problem when you have children. Mothers and fathers are so diligent when they are around their children, saying things like "That god-damn—I mean gosh darn—delivery boy! When is he going to get our paper here on time!" or "Shit—Shoot—I can't believe I just dropped an anvil on my foot, it hurts like hell—I mean heck." And when you are around their kids, they expect you to be equally careful, omitting all potentially offensive words from your speech. I have always complied to the best of my ability, but it has never quite made sense to me. I mean, what happens when a three-year-old says "Shit!" when she is frustrated, other than the little titillation she enjoys because she knows she is trying to get away with something she is not supposed to do? I'll tell you what happens: one thing. The parent gets embarrassed. If other parents are around, he thinks that the other parents will think ill of him because he has allowed his child to swear. As though he is a bad, loose parent because of it. That's it. He is just trying to save face in front of other parents. It's not that he really doesn't want his child to swear, it's that he doesn't want to look bad because of it. It's all an ego thing, as just about everything in parenting turns out to be.

It is hard to find parents of like minds. You like to assume that people who you think think like you actually do think like you, but when you test it out, you could be ever so wrong. It's like ragging on Richard Nixon to a mother in the park who is wearing Birkenstocks, only to have her say, "Hey, Dick was the best president we've had this century! He did what they all do, he just got caught is all." Who would've thunk? Swearing is the same thing. You throw a few good ones around in the telling of an innocent story only to find out that you are talking to a cardinal in layman's clothing.

And, of course, you are just putting off the inevitable. A college-age child is free to say what he or she likes, as is an older high-school kid. So where does one start loosening the guidelines between the ages of two and sixteen? If they are going to do it anyway, why not just let it rip from the very beginning? But, I've been told, it's just ugly to hear the word "fuck" come out of the mouth of a five-year-old. This may be true. However, in some cases I find it side-splittingly funny and thereby worth its weight in entertainment value alone. As my daughter is picking up about five new words a day lately, and I have never bothered to curb my truck-driver verbal impulses, it was inevitable that the two would intersect sooner or later. Yesterday, it happened. She came up to me and said "Sit!"

"Sit?" I said, trying to figure out what she was saying.

"Sit!" she repeated as I racked my brain. Now, normally, it takes only a split second for a mother to translate a passing look on her child's face to mean "I am hungry and I want to eat cream cheese on toast with banana and chocolate syrup, but since you said we were out of chocolate syrup yesterday, how about pancakes?" and be dead on the money. This astounds the nonparents in the room. It even astounds the father at times. A child can be reading a book with Daddy when she all of a sudden says "No!" to the mystified dad, who is holding her on his lap. It just takes a Mom to step in on occasion to tell Dad that she doesn't like that page because there is no picture of Cookie Monster on it and besides that, she is blinking her left eye, which means that she really wants to read Mother Goose, which she calls Gooz, but only after getting a drink of milk, which you can obviously tell by the way she is holding her right big toe apart from her other toes. To which Dad will silently wonder about just what goes on in the house when he is away at work all day. So when my daughter came up to me and said, "Sit!" I had to pause for longer than my usual microsecond to figure out what she meant, just like when she walked around the house saying "Jew! Jew! Jew!" and I wondered if she could possibly mean that she was damn proud of her heritage until I finally figured out that she meant that she wanted to go to the zoo.

I knew that she didn't want to sit down, because when she wants to sit she says "Seat!" Then it dawned on me.

"Shit?" I asked, looking at her closely.

"Ya. Sit!" She smiled with the pride of being able to make herself clearly understood. I had to laugh. It was hilarious. Then I spilled a huge glass of milk and without thinking twice shouted, "God *damn* it!" after which she went walking around the house saying "Gettammed, gettammed." And frankly, I didn't stop her. Maybe when she walks around saying "Fuck this! I can't stand all these goddamn shitty toys. And by the way, you're in a particularly bitchy mood today, which frankly, Mother, I could do without," I will eat my words. But for now, a little "Sit!" and "Gettammed" puts a real smile on my face.

I know that I am virtually alone in my attitude about this problem, and I can hear more experienced parents cluck their tongues and shake their heads as they read this, thinking to themselves, "She is *so* deluded. Just wait till that kid is five or six and walking around her first-grade class saying 'I cannot eat one more goddamn goldfish for a snack or I am going to go fucking crazy!' and the principle calls her at work to talk about what is going on at home, she gets a visit from the Child Welfare Department, and all the other kids' parents stop inviting her to birthday parties and play dates. She is going to be changing her tune real fast. All that stuff that is cute and adorable now? It'll come back to haunt her, mark my words. Does she even realize how bad she is fucking this child up? I certainly hope she is saving for therapy as well as for college."

So, prepare yourself for a life of socializing with people not because you find them scintillating intellects, but because they Ferberize (or don't Ferberize). Not because they have a lust for life and work toward the betterment of humanity, but because they will give up their rules on organic food long enough to let a kid enjoy a piece of cake on his birthday—frosting too! Cloth diapers can really cement a bond. So can ear infections, home schooling, aversions to antibiotics, and breast-feeding till the child opens his first checking account. You'll find yourself breaking down barriers and erecting new ones unexpectedly. And the next thing you know, the mom in the park wearing Birkenstocks and worshipping Richard Nixon will be your best friend because she is out at the park at the same time every day, has children the same age as yours who have had the same number of ear infections and share the same pediatrician, and, oh yeah, mashes up her own baby food (seeing as how this is her first child. By number two or three, it's Taco Bell daily). Just don't mention Watergate.

TOILET TALK

Men can read maps better than women.
'Cause only the male mind could conceive of
one inch equaling a hundred miles.

—ROSEANNE

THE FIRST TIME I BOUGHT

a potty seat for my daughter, she sat down on it and pooped.

When she was done, she stood up, looked at the potty, and started toddling around the bathroom looking for something more interesting to do. Now, I don't read this as some indication of genius on her part, that maybe, since she has some natural ability to do what she needs to do where she needs to do it without a line of cheerleaders or absurd incentives (a Beanie Baby for every poop, say), she will break 1300 on her SATs. No. I am happy, thrilled, in fact, that it looks like this may not be a huge issue in our household, but again, this is not what really stops me in my tracks about this minor miracle. What makes me want to kvell about it, call my relatives and friends and tell them in gory detail, has nothing to do with timing or smarts. It has to do with the fact that there was no sports page involved whatsoever.

Girls make sense to me. When they go into the bathroom alone, they do what they need to do, and move on with their day, week, lives. They don't sit there for a half hour, unable to relax their sphincter muscles without reading about Kirby Puckett's glaucoma, Steve Young's relation to Brigham, or who beat who in the playoffs, which they already saw on television as they happened. Now, I can see reaching out for a catalog or a magazine to pass the time if you have to sit for more than a minute or two (and how often do you *really* have to do that?). But to bring reading material *with* you, as though it were a library, and be unable to make any progress without it seems to me to be the very essence of absurdity. What is it about reading that helps one move one's bowels? Female bowels seem to need far less coaxing. I never have to ask a man why he's leaving the room if he has reading material in his hand, because it is painfully obvious that he is heading up to the bathroom. And from what I've seen, it doesn't exactly have to be Homer to qualify. The last thing I saw going upstairs in my house was the Sunday throwaway section of the paper advertising sales on lawn tools, paint thinner, and birdseed. Scintillating!

Why and when did reading become an Olympic bathroom event? Can we not sit for a moment without doing something? Are there toilets in the library stacks? When did reading even get associated with bodily waste? Do you think the Egyptian pharaohs chose their dumping ground on the basis of its proximity to the most interesting set of hieroglyphics? Maybe so, but I'm sure the Nefertitis were shrugging and rolling their eyes just like their modern-day counterparts.

Last I knew, the object of going to the bathroom (alone) was to go to the bathroom. Not to catch up on the last issue of *National Geographic* that came to your house, review Martha Stewart's recipe for a homemade mud mask, or study for a correspondence course in cartooning. Is a hard, cold, ceramic stool

so much more comfortable than, say, a chaise longue that anyone would actually choose it as a preferred reading spot?
Frankly, a smelly bathroom is the very last place I would think
about for curling up with a good book, and I fail to see how anyone would think that reading there would be relaxing or helpful
in any way. And in fact, in my house, when things really get
competitive and we start arguing about who did what and who
does more around the house and Paul starts saying, "I'm getting to it!" I feel compelled to shout, "Well, if you spent half the
time straightening up that you do reading box scores, we could
be living in a museum by now!" I think the whole problem
could be solved if men just ate a lot more fruit in the morning.

Of course, some men will confess that the time they spend
reading in the bathroom is the only downtime they get, their
only time to be alone. That if they step outside the confines of
the bathroom, already respected as a place for privacy, then
their time is not their own, they are asked to do things all the
time, and they will never get a tiny break to even catch up on
Dennis Rodman's new hair color. I like that one a lot. This,
while he is out running a few times a week, going to the
health club here and there, and buying tickets to an occasional
basketball game while you do things like organize the linen
closet, clip your child's nails (has a man ever done that anywhere in the world?), put photos in an album, and look for
sippy cups that really don't leak. Call me competitive, that is
the way I see things. Not that men don't come by their toilet
obsessions naturally, I actually think they do.

From an early age, boys seem to find bodily functions so
utterly engrossing, they think that everyone else should as well.
They think it's hilarious, we think it's disgusting. Perhaps it is
genetic, or maybe just a manly ritual passed down from father to

son in some unspoken law of behavior. Nature versus nurture as applied to the loo. My own father never took reading material into the bathroom, but that is mostly because it wasn't on his list, and if it wasn't on his list, it didn't happen (or else he just did it too early in the morning for anyone to notice—after his 5:30 feeding of the cat, his 5:34 cup of espresso, and his 5:39 exercises).

When it comes to bathroom etiquette, men know no shame. Unfortunately you do not find this out until you live with one. Men seem to be deaf, blind, and without any olfactory function whatsoever as soon as they cross the bathroom threshold. They unabashedly do what they have to do regardless of what sounds they are making and their proximity to another person or a group of people. In my in-laws' house, there is a small bathroom right off the kitchen/dining room. Actually, it is *in* the kitchen/dining room. Now, when you are in this bathroom, you can hear someone breathing in the next room, so it is safe to assume that they can hear you floss your teeth, let alone suffer gastrointestinal duress. A woman would sooner talk about her nipple hairs to a stranger on the train than use that bathroom while other people were in the kitchen or dining room (unless she was just going in to wash her hands or, at *most*, pee). The men in the family, however, think nothing of just going right in there and letting it all out, regardless of who is around, proving the oft-aired theory that men find it difficult to see how their needs should somehow go delayed, deferred, or at least muffled a little. I know women who will run the faucet just so you won't hear them *peeing.* I've known women to use a bathroom on a different floor, in a different department, and even then to wait until it's empty to use it if they think they will somehow embarrass themselves with unseemly noises. One time, I had an upset stomach while at the dinner party of some friends. Their bathroom was embarrassingly close to the dining room, so I quietly went upstairs to do what I needed to. When I came down, the host, a male, said to me loudly, "What did you go upstairs for? There is a bathroom right there!" This is a question a woman would never ask. In fact, a woman can be suffering from dysentery, the stomach flu, and twisted intestines, and she will still pass gas in utter silence. This is what she has trained herself to do. A man so much as eats a brussels sprout and he is a human jet pack. Is it any wonder the divorce rate is so high?

The other night Paul thought the baby was choking and scrambled out of bed, running to the baby, who, it turned out, was fine. In the morning I asked him, "And what would you do if she was choking?" Long pause.

"I don't know, probably yell for you."

"That's what I figured. You should read that *Pediatric Life Support* book we have."

"Where is it?"

"In the bathroom."

"In the bathroom?"

"Yes. Because I thought that was my best shot at getting you to read it." He was embarrassed, but had to admit that my logic was sound.

Bathroom reading is one of the hardest habits to break a man of. It's like some proud display of their manhood. I know men who would sooner wear an apron, do the ironing, pick out fabric, and whip together a banana flambé than give up their bathroom pleasures. This mystifies me. But they just counter this attack with the age-old argument about women who spend too much time in the bathroom getting ready or "God knows what." Well, God isn't the only one who knows what, I know what. Women may spend time in the bathroom, but it isn't reading while they are on the pot (most of them). They are generally doing one of three things (other than cleaning it): getting ready, talking to friends, or getting depressed. Let's take these one at a time.

Getting ready: I personally don't take long to get ready, so get off my back. I am in and out like a light, as they say, since I don't blow-dry the hair, apply any makeup, or wear anything that requires panty hose.

Talking to friends: As I mentioned once before, juicy conversations must not be interrupted merely because one has to take a tinkle. Or blow her nose or get ready for some event. This is busy work compared to the art of conversation. One woman will be in the shower while the other is sitting on the toilet talking to her. Perfectly natural. This is where some of the best talking gets done. Plus, it is a great place to collect opinions about moisturizers, earring choices, and panty shields.

Getting depressed: Here is where the bathroom is Queen. There is no more perfect place to inspire a downward spiral than a room whose sole purpose is to provide an avenue for you to look at yourself from any one of a dozen angles. God help you if you have a full-length or a three-way. Looking in the mirror is a daunting task and can even get to a girl who is in the cheeriest of moods on a beautiful spring day when the windows are wide open and the stereo is blasting Earth, Wind & Fire. The strongest of us can crumble and often do. It's hard to face ourselves naked and blemished—sad but true. How I would love to be able to embrace every inch, but let's face it, who's got arms that long? It's a sad state of affairs when one has to watch one's mutinous body as it starts gathering up all its flesh and heading south for the winter, to say nothing of the rest of your life.

ON BECOMING A FRUMP

I'm tired of all this nonsense about beauty
being only skin deep. That's deep enough.
What do you want, an adorable pancreas?
—JEAN KERR

THE FIRST TIME YOU GET

pregnant, you feel magical. The second time you get pregnant, you feel like a tour bus—so big, you can't see your own rear end, unless you're turning a corner. And it isn't any one particular thing that puts you over the edge, because they all creep up on you so quietly, like, maybe, so many tarantulas. The jelly belly, the spider veins, the dry flaky skin that looks like your gams have been stored in the freezer for a month with no cling wrap . . . you know the drill. No, it's never just one symptom, because any one of them is acceptable in and of itself as a natural indicator of the aging process. But all together, it is too much to bear. You are forced to realize that you have crossed over the line you vowed never to get near. You don't just look like a mother, you have a mother's *body*. In short, you have become a frump.

Becoming a frump is one of the benchmarks of maturity that is hardest for a girl to accept. First and foremost, it is unsightly. And one hates to think of oneself as unsightly.

Prior to becoming a frump, it was pretty easy to disguise one or two figure flaws. A cinched waist, a baggy sweater, shoulder pads were always good (provided they were sewn into the lining of the garment and thereby invisible. Nothing is more pathetic than shoulder pads that show. *Très gauche*). But allover frumpiness, that is a challenge too great for even the best makeover artist. There are always exceptions to the rule, but these are aliens, so we don't have to account for them because they just lower our curve. Actually, my sisters are two of those people. One sister has three children, is over forty, and looks better than she did twenty years ago. My other sister, two kids and runs eight miles at a stretch. I've never understood it. Bizarre. But I have to forgive them because they are family. The rest of the world is not so lucky.

A mother's body is what a young girl looks at with awe and disgust. She is awed at what it has been through, but disgusted at the price it has paid. She sees the size of the underwear in her mother's drawer, its boxlike shape, nylon feel, and astonishing net-weight capacity, and she goes running from the room. I mean, she loves her mother and adores her mother's body, but lives in fear of the dark road that leads from here to there. When someone compliments her mother on something that she is wearing, or the weight she has recently lost, the daughter brims with pride—but then secretly wonders what they would say if they saw her in her nylons and bra, getting ready for a party.

So it's a little hard to swallow waking up to find that the underwear in your own drawer has gone from bikini brief to your basic mailbag. And the little dimples that speckled your upper thighs have now spread like poison ivy to your knees, hips, and upper arms. You know you have truly arrived as a frump when you will consider a bathing suit only if it has a skirt and built-in cups.

And while it is bad enough watching your body melt into middle age by yourself, or with your husband, who tries to be consoling (but look at him, is not the pot calling the kettle plump?), the absolute worst thing, the very very worst part about it, is having a daughter and knowing that one day, in just a few years, she will be sitting on the toilet top, watching you get dressed for a party, maybe advising you on these earrings versus those, and she will suddenly realize that your body is really, really gross. Disgusting, even. That it is stretched out and saggy and looks nothing like anything she wants anything to do with. She is going to look at you and for the first time, instead of loving you blindly and wanting to be just like you in every way, she will start to rethink her whole image of you in her head and it won't change until she is approaching her own midlife, and by then, of course, you will be convalescing at Whispering Pines, where Mary the day nurse will be offering you stewed prunes and tapioca.

This is as tough a pill to swallow as any. It is enough to drive a woman to excess. Excess cheesecake, excess truffles, excess Klondikes. While it is not like her to give up, it is too daunting a task in the face of mothering young children to try and maintain any control over any part of your life whatsoever, let alone chip away at the body that defies all logic, like a failed human soufflé where half has sunken in and half has overflowed.

And while I am all for good health and proper eating and climbing stairs without changing elevation, I'm not even sure if it's dignified for a person my age to be lithe and taut, though there *may* be a happy medium between that and having a permanent girth equal to that of a hula hoop.

I have now come to see my stomach as a symbol, a tribute, a living testament to the cycle of life, the essence of man's existence, like a soft, yeasty commemorative statue. And as such, like a historical monument, it shouldn't be tinkered with. Instead it should be celebrated as a masterpiece of nature.

Isn't this the way a mother should look? Isn't it a prerequisite for membership? Wouldn't I rather show my daughter the way it really is than to put the added pressure on her of having a really sexy mom? Nothing could be worse than that. So I figure it this way: I'm doing it for her. I will be no threat whatsoever to her budding sprig of a body. Not that it's easy or that I am particularly happy to have three chins, but what is a mother's life for if not gut-wrenching sacrifice? She may be horrified at a young age, but she will thank me later. And now I can mentally prepare myself for a life in dresses with the fashion allure of a shower cap. And when I feel the urge, sometime in the next decade or so, to join a health club and lose some weight, I will stop myself cold and remember what's best for the children.

BEAUTY AND THE BREAST

(AND OTHER TITBITS)

My Playtex Living Bra died—of starvation.
—PHYLLIS DILLER

LET'S NOT STOP THERE.
After adjusting to the heartache that has replaced your stomach, a girl would be wise to put black tape on her mirror at breast level so that she may never again have to face the stocking caps of flesh that have taken root where her breasts once were.

I don't even have breasts anymore. They're more like Tater Tits. Tiny, lifeless blobs of fat that look like they took a running dive off my chest and never quite made it to the floor. And it depresses me every time I look at them, not because they are such pathetically wilted reminders of what was once a pretty nice bloom and not because they remind me that my body is just a nipple hair away from my mother's body, which I used to stare at in amazement wondering what had happened to her to make her look like that—no, what gets me deep inside my soul is that my breasts just seem so *spiritless*. Lifeless. Spent. Depressed.

Without the benefit of surgery, I have had many different sized breasts in my life. Gain and lose enough weight and you too can experience everything from Twiggy to Dolly. When I was prepubescent and my breasts were the size of Hershey's Kisses, I was too oblivious to care. I just watched my sister buy padded bras and wondered what was in store for me. Then, by the time things shook out (of course, I took care not to have that literally happen), I looked okay. Nothing to flaunt, nothing to brag about, nothing to attract unwanted attention, but at the same time, more than a Hershey's Kiss. Small but upright. Something in the biscuit family, if you cared to look.

Then, toward the end of high school, I woke up one day and found I'd gained twenty pounds and two casabas. Which was something to get used to. But in those days I was disciplined enough to take the weight off without waiting for the next decade to pass, so it wasn't much of a problem. Then, a few years later, I started the Early Twenties Downward Spiral, spent all my free time at Dairy Queen drowning in chocolate chip banana blizzards, and pretty soon I couldn't stand on my head without smothering in my own flesh. My breasts preceded me wherever I went, announcing to the world that the rest of me was soon to follow. Working out was like an exercise in animal training. I just wanted to stand on a chair, whip in hand, and scream, "Down, girls!" They were constantly in the way. Shirts didn't fit, bras were uncomfortable, and turning around suddenly could knock me flat. And worst of all, when I was naked at the end of a long day, quietly expanding in the safety of my own bathrobe, my breasts could be felt on something I'd never anticipated: my stomach. My torso had just sort of folded in on itself, sweating between the cracks.

But eventually I got it under control, and my breasts no longer occupied my lap at all times. I enjoyed a brief period of rotundity without moribundity. Until I got pregnant. I should have been tipped off when my breasts became like bloated black-and-blue cannonballs affixed to my chest. I couldn't sleep on my stomach without a pillow carefully elevating me so that no part of my breast so much as touched the mattress. I finally just took to wearing my bra to bed.

The only sign I had that a new life was growing within was the pain without. Jiggling of any kind sent me reeling. Walking down stairs was painful. Driving over potholes, excruciating. And I thought I had died and gone to heaven when the pain subsided three months later. Then I had a few months' respite when my breasts went back to being my old friends, soft, round, and familiar.

Then one day, about eight months in, something actually started coming out of them.

Now, all your life you know that your nipple is supposed to be a little spigot. That its whole purpose in life, in fact, is to be a big tap when your breast becomes a big keg. But when you go thirty-five years seeing them as just pinkish-brown things that point the rest of your breast in the right direction, it's a little weird when you actually see them function like they were made to. I mean, how many times have I looked down at myself in the shower and wondered, So, where *exactly* is it supposed to come out?

And then, of course, it happened. My baby was born. And let me tell you, my milk didn't "come in" like they told me in all the books, it stormed my chest like a tidal wave running up against Hoover Dam. Now my breasts were so engorged, they were as taut as Nancy Reagan sucking on a lemon, and twice as hard. The skin was stretched so tightly over them I could practically see my own heart beating. I was a fountain of milk. And the only thing between the ocean that sat between my shoulders and my hungry little babe was my poor defenseless nipples—now the size of sausage patties—that not only act as little locks but chewing toys as well. You may as well give your toothless baby some Naugahyde, she would do less damage. Soreness, blisters, and finally, hamburger meat. Feeding a baby with sore nipples is like getting a titty twister from Edward Scissorhands. And once the tears are streaming down your cheeks when she latches on, you know you've arrived. The breast is doing what it does best. Your nipple has elongated into a bendy straw. Your baby is not only chewing you raw, she is constantly grabbing your breast with both hands like she is steering a gigantic bus. Still, they are doing the work of the four basic food groups and burning up extra calories to boot. What could be bad?

The end result. Tiny, lifeless blobs of fat that look like they took a running leap off my chest and never quite made it to the floor. And unfortunately, I think that is where they're going to stay. A golf ball hanging in a sweat sock has a nicer shape than I. Some people say it comes back. I say they are liars. Some people say, look at your mother and you'll know how you'll turn out. I say, do I have to? I guess I shouldn't complain. I mean, they've served me well. But it makes me have second thoughts about more children. If this is what one little guy did to them, what would happen after two, three, or God forbid, four? I shudder to think. Good-bye, Old Glory, hello, Hershey's Kiss.

DOWN THERE

Nobody's interested in sweetness and light.
—HEDDA HOPPER

I HAVE A FRIEND WHO HAS four nieces. Needless to say, theirs is a very female-centric household. And the single funniest line I have ever heard uttered anywhere, ever, came out of the mouth of one of her nieces at the age of three or so. Her dad was walking around the house naked, as he was wont to do, and she suddenly turned to her mother and said, "Mommy, what's that thing hanging out of Daddy's vagina?"

An astute girl, that three-year-old (later, when her father was teasing her about a diaper that was hanging too low, calling out, "Plumber butt, plumber butt!" she turned to him and said, "No, Daddy, it's plumber *vagina*"). I think I was in fifth grade before I even knew what a vagina was, let alone which sex had one. I mean, what it really was. I knew that there were folds of skin that were *called* the vagina, but as far as an actual bodily opening that leads to further reproductive organs, this was only a pink stalk of billowy tissue on the pages of science books. I didn't make the connection between that and my own anatomy for years. And that's a good thing. First, because ignorance is bliss, and second, because it is such a hubbub of

activity later in life that the more time it has to rest and prepare, the better.

Think about it. By the time a woman has had a baby or
two, there's been enough traffic around there to warrant a
stoplight. If only it were that simple. Imagine being on a date
with someone whose advances you could ward off with a simple "Sorry, I'd love to, Bill, but as you can see, you've gotten a
red light. Bad timing, better luck next time!" as you collect
your things and scamper out the door.

Because the vagina serves as the Grand Central of our bodies, beginning with the old menstruation express that passes
through early on, I think it is the heart, the foundation, the very
essence of why women are a much tougher lot than men. We
bleed from it every month. Our threshold of pain is much
higher, our tolerance for invasive procedures is necessarily
greater, and let's just say that our all-around martyr complex is
inconsequential compared to those of "others we know." A
woman could be balancing two young children with eight bags
of groceries in subzero temperatures while maintaining a rag-
ing strep throat, pneumonia, and athlete's foot and you won't
hear a peep out of her. If a man has a frog in his throat, he
won't stop whining until you find him the lozenges, since his
eyes were recently gouged out and he can no longer see to look
for them. And the smartest of men, the Ph.D. nuclear physi-
cist–astronaut–brain surgeon, has the IQ of a three-year-old
when it comes to taking care of himself (or anyone else, I might
add). He could be throwing up all night and sit down to a breakfast of bacon, eggs, pancakes, and cream-style corn, and when
you look at him skeptically he will look at you with all sincerity
and say, "What? Are the eggs bad for me?" There is only so
much of this a woman can take. When my daughter was a few

weeks old I developed mastitis, a painful breast infection that presents itself with flulike symptoms that make you feel like the walking dead, a fever, and a painful, hard lump in the already tender nursing breast. Nevertheless, I took care of her, nursed her in great pain, changed her, played with her, rocked her, did the dishes, tried to sleep, but got up when she got up and did the whole thing all over again. My husband gets a runny nose and asks if it can be a sign of Ebola. What happened to the stoic male? The macho man? He falls to pieces at the slightest sign of illness. A headache is immediately thought to be an inoperable brain tumor, a backache a sure sign of a degenerative muscular disorder, and a new mole, fatal carcinoma. The other day Paul actually said to me, pointing to a tiny red patch on his finger, "Do you think this could be frostbite?" "Gee, I don't know," I answered. "Have you been scaling Mount Everest lately?" and handed him the Vaseline Intensive Care. It is no wonder that women have little pity for men's bellyaching while they are ill. As it is, I am convinced that if men did most of the carrying of car seats, the seats would be made out of titanium and sleekly designed to avoid disc slippage.

I trace this all back to the menstrual period, as I mentioned. It is here that young women are trained in the art of tolerance, since cleaning up after your body's involuntary processes is not always pleasant, but a task that we endure without a whole lot of fuss (to say nothing of the spit-up, throw-up, poop, pee, snot, and diaper rash of the kids we babysit). And it is at this juncture in a girl's development, while she is figuring out whether she requires slender regular, regular, super, or torpedo, that we see the beginning of the aforementioned traffic jam, with bodily fluids and tampons competing for a very small space. Standing room only.

Later on, it could be a finger or two, and let's not forget our good friend the speculum, that sort of shoe tree for the vagina. Medical device or instrument of torture? And along with the speculum, of course, comes a lubricant and a swab. Of course, if the swab finds anything abnormal, they bring in the heavier artillery, and all you can hope for is a little sign you can hang at the entrance that reads GONE FISHING.

Then there are always the invaders, the uninvited guests like yeast. (I would like to see a male CEO sit through a business meeting with a secret yeast infection. Before the cost-benefit analysis, the paramedics would be summoned.) Here, I think, we can add medication to the vagina-invader list—medication that requires an applicator and, like everything else in the vagina, falls victim to gravity and naturally spills out. Another mess to clean up.

Next we can move on to the world of the penis and its introduction to the well-worn vagina. Here, the varieties are too numerous to mention. Just suffice it to say that they never come alone (no pun intended). Well, they do if they are made out of plastic, another very viable alternative. But if you want one in the flesh, then you have to deal with all its accoutrements. If a penis's owner is responsible, then it comes with a condom. If not, add a diaphragm and jelly to the list, or maybe a surgically inserted IUD. Then there are always even more bodily fluids to deal with. Is it really possible that there is anything left to fertilize an egg when so much of that goo trickles down your innards and out into the world? I have not yet decided if ours is one of the most ingenious designs in the universe or one of the most idiotic. But do let's move on.

So far, we have a traffic flow of blood, bodily fluids, tampons, specula, swabs, yeast, medication, fingers, penises, and birth-control devices, to which list we add babies. A baby would be the largest object to pass through even the most tolerant vagina. Thank God it has only to go one way. The whole reproductive thing is akin to a human ship in a bottle. It goes in small, gets built up, and then you basically have to break it open to get it out. (At my six-week check after having my first child, the midwife gave me her some-women-have-problems-with-lubrication-after-birth spiel and wrote the name of a product she highly recommended for just such a problem, should I encounter it: "Astroglide." I looked at her. *"Astroglide?"* I said. "You've got to be kidding me." "Nope," she said. "Try it." And then she leaned in close, lowered her voice, and, with a sparkle in her eye, she smiled slyly. "It's heavenly." There you have it. Astroglide. Another item for the list.) In the span of a woman's lifetime, there comes a time when she just wants to pull up the drawbridge that says NO TRESPASSING or NO SOLICITING or, more simply put, GO AWAY.

But by then it is too late. The baby is getting older and now all you have to do is answer its every need, day or night. And then, before you know it, you will be looking forward to hormone-replacement therapy, which will leave you in sanitary pads for the rest of your life. But that shouldn't be a problem for you. You are strong. You are invincible. Or at least you would be, if only you could get a little sleep under your belt—and leave the rest of what's under your belt alone.

ONE MORE WORD ABOUT THE PENIS, OR, BOY, OH BOY

May your every wish be granted.
—ANCIENT CHINESE CURSE

I HAVE A PENIS IN ME.

Deep inside. It probably only measures about a sixteenth of an inch, but I'm not complaining. Can a girl in my situation be so picky? I know what you're thinking, and please, get your mind out of the gutter, for God's sake. What do you think I am, some kind of pervert who takes time out from a sexual tryst to tell the world what is happening blow by blow (no pun intended) just to heighten the appeal of my book? Really.

I'm talking about another kind of penis. Another kind altogether. The kind on a growing baby in the deep recesses of my body, due to come out on New Year's Eve. One that is attached to little boy legs and little boy arms and a big boy belly and a little boy face whose topography I can only dream about in the most misty of ways. This is a representative body part, one that will someday be a plaything, a source of fascination, an obsession, and finally just another body part. But to know that there is a boy inside my belly is to be forced to think about boys in general and how to raise the one who will

stand apart from the rest of his sex in his sheer well-rounded-
ness, maturity, good listening ability, sensitivity, confidence,
graciousness, and utter unmalelike behavior—in short, how
to raise a real mensch. After all, how often do you get the
chance to start from scratch?

The decision to find out the sex of an unborn child is
always a tricky one. Some people, of course, don't agonize
over the decision; they know what they want. That wouldn't be
me. These are confident people who can make decisions easily and not be haunted by them for months, years, or decades.
They either feel that they want to be surprised, as Mother
Nature intended us to be, or they want to know what color to
paint the nursery, so do tell. For me, as usual, it was a little
more complicated. With my first baby, I found out inadvertently that I was having a girl. Since I had moved from one
part of the country to another in the middle of my pregnancy
and had not chosen a new doctor yet, my old doctor sent my
medical records to me (what a novel thought, you get to see
your own medical records!). Now, I don't know about you, but
when a two-inch stack of papers comes to the house, a two-
inch stack of papers about nothing but me, I am not going to
get up from my chair until I have read every last document
and found out what all my doctors have been saying about me
all these years. Could there be anything more alluring? No.
(Maybe an ex-lover's diary, but what men keep diaries? Actually, I did secretly look at one guy's diary when he was out of
the house one day, but when I found myself reading sentences like "Thank you Jesus for the great coffee this morning," I decided that I could not reconcile this sentiment with
the delusion I was enjoying about my compatibility with this
man and shut the book immediately.) So as I sat there reading

about every pap smear I ever endured, I unwittingly came across the results of an amniocentesis I had had and read a statement that said, "XX, typical female genotype." At first, I was confused—I thought they meant me. Then I realized that I was going to have a baby girl and went leaping around the house (I have six nephews). And for me, knowing that it was a girl, despite the fact that technology has enabled us to know things that sometimes I wish we had no capability of knowing, was great. You spend so much of your first pregnancy wondering just who this person is, what it'll look like, whether it'll be covered with tattoos by the time it's sixteen, et cetera, that being able to relate to this child in just one simple, concrete way made a difference for me. So I thought that this time around, I want to know again. Then they told me it was a boy. A boy! I will be raising a *boy*. Some day there will be one guy walking around on this earth, just one guy in a sea of millions, whom I actually had some influence on. A guy you get to mold right from the start, not come into the picture after twenty-five years when he chews with his mouth open, blow-dries his hair, and insists on a girlfriend whose hips could slip through a keyhole without a scratch. And if I can raise a great guy, the greatest guy, who will go out and father more greatest guys, then the pebble of my existence will have a little ripple in the world.

Knowing much more about girls than boys, I immediately assume that it will be harder to raise a wonderful man, because of the sheer number of yahoos I have come into contact with over the years. Even though I realize that girls are no treat come the age of thirteen or so, that they spend a good ten years hating their mothers and being wildly embarrassed that their mothers are even living here on this earth, I still think that despite their moments (maybe generations) of temporary insanity, they usually come out on the other end as fascinating, well-rounded, insightful, resilient creatures. Guys, while easier to deal with in the adolescent years, have all the outside influences in the whole world egging them on to act like putzes. What could be worse than having no one to blame but yourself for contributing to the jerkiness of yet one more guy in the world? Nothing! So this is the opportunity of a lifetime, the chance to get things right. To teach this little one to do the dishes as well as unclog the drain. To encourage him to be sensitive, but also secretly feed his mischievous side so he has a hint of bad-boyness within. To make sure that he knows how to properly fold a towel, even if it is after whipping it at someone's butt in the locker room.

This is a daunting task. Millions of women have been given this assignment before and failed miserably, and if millions have failed before me, what on earth makes me think that I can do any better?

Maybe you are doomed before you start. Maybe forgetting birthdays, not returning phone calls, and failing to realize that a wet, crumpled towel on the bathroom floor will eventually start to mildew and stink up the whole house are genetic, and there really is no hope. However, the geneticist I talked to never said, in reviewing all the possible genetic abnormalities that can occur, "Oh, and by the way, if it's a boy, you know that genetically speaking your chances are more than ninety-eight percent that he will be a jerk in some way." So I think we can knock off genetics as the source of the problem.

In all fairness, I will say that I don't think you have to do things a lot differently when trying to raise a girl mensch than you do a boy mensch, with the possible exception of making sure that the toilet seat stays down, yet the differences between men and women are a gaping chasm there for all to see. If I smother him with love as I plan to, will I be sowing the seeds of a latent fear of intimacy? If I don't, will he be insecure and spend a lifetime lusting after any kook who will love him? The margin of error here is just too great not to make you feel like you're doomed before the baby has even taken his first breath. I mean, is it fair to expect that the same person who can leap tall buildings in a single bound and run faster than a speeding bullet would also be able to recognize that a paisley tie doesn't go with a powder-blue checked shirt? Or is that really just too much to ask? Not for my guy, since he will, of course, be the exception to every rule. The carpenter who is a gourmet cook, keeps house immaculately, and would never break up with a gal in the middle of the night after a roll in the hay. The CEO who is building his own log cabin in the woods and hunts for his own food, living completely off the land. The Wall Street analyst who founds a center for disadvantaged youth and single-handedly turns around the lives of thousands of children, while at the same time practicing yoga to get in touch with his physical being, still finding the time to iron his wife's blouse for work the next day. That kind of thing. Yes, this little child will be every woman's dream date, with a heart as big as Texas and an intellect as far reaching as Cassiopeia, and all this will be achieved in his perfect, pressure-free household where everything works like a Swiss watch.

Hah! I can hear the men with the straitjacket pulling up now. Don't think I don't know that I am deluding myself in so grand a way as to appear imbalanced to any mental-health professional worth her salt. I know that. But isn't that every woman's job, to delude herself about her own children? In fact, isn't that one of the payoffs to all the pain of childbirth, the exhaustion of infancy, the exhaustion of the toddler years, the exhaustion of the grade-school years, and the anguish and misery of adolescence? I should hope so. There have to be some rewards along the way. I think that self-deception and delusional thinking are perfect candidates. So, off I go, thinking that I will be able to guide, nurture, and love my children so that piercing their nipples never even crosses their minds. I will support them so that their adolescence flies by unnoticed, barely a blip on life's continuum. There will be one of each sex, so they will lack the treasure of a sibling of the same sex, but by the same token I will not have to referee any fights over the blow-dryer. They will, of course, get along so well that he will teach her to be a fantastic fielder (since the one time I played on a softball team and was out in the field ready to catch an important fly ball, the ball hit the edge of my glove, bounced off, and hit me in the face, giving me a massive shiner and the other team a run. Can I help it if the sun was particularly blinding that day?) and she will make sure he treats his girlfriends right and beat him bloody if he doesn't. She will be confident and happy and never think twice about being fat. She won't be ruled by what boys think of her and will never sport blue eye shadow. She will be mature beyond her years but never lose her fun-loving, childlike spontaneity. He will not cave to the macho behavior of the tougher boys and will have sympathy for all the boys who don't fit in. He will be confident and happy and contemplate greater issues than whether the Bulls will ever regain their dominance. At the same time, he will be able to knock around with the best of them, relating to all social sets from jocks to eggheads because he is so versatile and well rounded. Her friends will probably have crushes on him and his friends will think she's a dish. They will both take their place as the stars of the household, unfettered by the natural competition between same-sex siblings.

Moreover, since all roads ultimately lead to the mother, all the adults who cross their path will whisper as they pass, "Who raised those kids? They sure did a helluva job." And all the children who get to know them will say to them enviously, "I sure wish I had parents like yours." And my husband and I will take our place in the Parents Hall of Fame, giving autographs, smiling for the paparazzi, and waiting for the alarm clock to sound.

EPILOGUE

Inside every older person is a younger person
wondering what happened.

———Jennifer Unlimited

It wasn't new year's

Eve, it was Christmas Eve. I woke up December 24 at one A.M.
I had a sinus infection and couldn't sleep. This was adding
insult to injury, waddling around ten months pregnant (the
nine-month thing is just the medical establishment's effort
not to scare you off. Pregnancy is forty weeks long. Divide by
four and you get ten. I rest my case) with a stuffed nose, green
snot, an achy head, and teeth that hurt. And then, at about
five-thirty, I started having contractions, by six they were getting fast, by seven we were at the hospital, and by nine he was
born. (See? women tell you their birthing stories whether you
want to hear them or not.) Another holiday child. The whole
thing was fast and furious, with a lot of nose blowing amid
the panting. My son came shooting out of me like a missile.
No time for laboring in the bathtub, no time for an epidural,
no time for so much as an aspirin.

"Did you scream like a wild animal?" my friend Bonnie asked.

"Like a wild animal being tortured slowly. They heard me
in Iowa."

"Congratulations," she said."You are now a Vaginal Warrior."

"I am?"

"You are. Welcome to the sisterhood."

Nice to know, I thought, that the only hall of fame I will ever make it into will be a vaginal one.

Now I am the mother of two, a shred of a human being. Exhausted, irritable, and so in love I can't look at a spring flower without collapsing in tears. Everyone told me after I had my daughter that one child was a vacation compared to two— and all I could do was walk around saying to myself, *This* is a vacation? But of course it was, and now life with one baby seems like a long nap on the beach. Simple, easy, beautiful. What I formerly thought of as sleep deprivation was like a shot of adrenaline by comparison. Shlepping one kid around while cranky? A cakewalk. Napping problems? No matter. Life with two puts life with one in the "good old days" category. Did I think I was resentful and grumpy, negative and critical before? Little Mary Sunshine compared to now. Homemakers of the fifties have become my new heroes. They did it with three, five, and seven kids, kept a perfectly clean house, cooked without microwaves, dressed without Velcro, and best of all, maintained a beehive with panache. You gotta hand it to them. They convinced me that offspring are why God created Valium.

In my old life, I used to fantasize about beautiful men. I used to fantasize about being on Broadway or in a Woody Allen movie.

Now, all I fantasize about is silence.

And solitude.

A vast abyss of nothingness. Hours and hours of no sound. A twenty-four-hour deprivation tank would be nirvana. No phone, no diaper changes, no one sucking at my breast, no Play-Doh to be removed from the floor, no one wanting milk in a sippy cup—no, water—no, milk—no laundry, no dishwasher to empty, no fingernails to clip, no cradle cap to pick at, no spit-up to clean off my shoulder, no badly designed car seats to carry around while my back slowly curves into a question mark, no dried-up glue stick under the couch, no spilled bubbles, no crushed Goldfish underfoot, no territorial disputes to referee.

But then I would have no tiny hands clasping my hair, no gummy smiles looking back at me, no belly to nibble, no windows into a brain where synapses are snap, crackle, and popping like firecrackers, no one wanting to hug me all day and kiss me all night, no one wanting to wear my earrings, no one growing before my very eyes, no one to laugh at every one of my jokes, no diaper changes, no one sucking at my breast, no Play-Doh to remove from the floor, no one wanting milk in a sippy cup—no, water—no, milk—no laundry, no dishwasher to empty, no fingernails to clip, no cradle cap to pick at, no spit-up to clean off my shoulder, no badly designed car seats to carry around while my back slowly curves into a question mark, no dried-up glue sticks under the couch, no spilled bubbles, no crushed Goldfish underfoot, no territorial disputes to referee.

And therein lies the rub.

When it comes to these pull-your-hair-out early years of child rearing, people say it gets easier. This too shall pass! The years fly by even if the days *never end*. And then, though it is horrifying to contemplate, one day the defining moments of their lives will no longer be *my* defining moments. This is too much for me to bear. Since I cry with abandon at GE commercials, you can only imagine the basket case I will be when it's their first day of school, their first slumber party, the first time they dance with (the twenty-first-century version of) Greg Alcoke, or their first boy–girl mixer (will they be among the fast kids in the closet?). Tomorrow I'll wake up and Ruby will be dating Deadheads (before she goes on to cure cancer) and Mo will be hiding a *Playboy* in the garage (before he goes on to negotiate world peace). This hits me when I dance around the living room with my little shmoodies and I actually have to hide my face so Ruby doesn't ask me why I'm crying to *Happy Tapping with Elmo.* I'd hate to sit her down and say, "You know, Ru, the circularity of life, the brevity of our time here on earth, and the heart-smashing strength of my love for you guys has just really gotten to me today." Since she is who she is, I'm sure she would understand, but I just hate to burden her at such a tender age. I don't even let myself think about things like when they are *gone* and the house is *empty.* Then what?

Then, of course, I will await my spiritual SWAT team to come and pick up the pieces. My trustees, my sounding boards, my confidantes, my royal advisors. I know that once the signal is sent, it won't take long for my girlfriends (now in their sixties) to be at the door and on the phone, ready with tea and sympathy and a vat of Chocolate Fudge Brownie. And we will do what we have done since Eve turned to Adam and said, "You're really nice and all, but aren't there any girls around here? I need a second opinion about this fig leaf." We will talk and talk and talk and shop and eat and hate people who are happier than we are and cry our eyes out and feel hopeless about our bodies, thinking to ourselves, You know, back when I was closing in on forty, I looked great compared to this! and worry about all the mistakes we might have made with our children, bemoan even more chin hair now that menopause has had its way with us, rag on our husbands now that we have had twenty more years to build up hostility and resentments, laugh at how neurotic we were in the early days, dance naked around the living room (only this time the shades will be drawn), take classes that we always wanted to take but never had the time for, and, of course, exchange hairstylists for the ever-important postrecovery pick-me-up. Then things won't be so bad when the dentist tells you he has to pull all your teeth, your husband buys a small red sports car and starts frequenting college bars, your therapist dies before you do, or your kids still hate you because of something you did twenty years before. Then a girl can cope. With her girlfriends in her back pocket, it's not just the defining moments that a woman can sink her ever-lovin' teeth into, it is the epic of the everyday, the monumental moments that go nowhere, the grist for the mill that just keeps grinding away. So, while you must live the life that you are going to live, and I would never presume to tell you how to go about such a daunting task, like most Jews, I do have a couple of recommendations: Close the book, lend it to your girlfriend (better yet, make her buy a copy at full price), and then unleash her astonishing proclivity toward complex analysis and advanced thinking, her searing powers of observation and insight, and ask her about her day.

ACKNOWLEDGMENTS

Thanks to my mother (who insisted I write this since she is the only one who will buy a hundred copies at full price; she has a point).

Every piece of work I've ever done has been, in small part, original, and in large part, so hugely influenced by my friends, editors, producers, colleagues, family, and demons, that it's hard to know where to begin when it comes to thanking them. Except the demons. Them, I'll skip.

There are six people, however, above all, without whom this book would never have been conceived, let alone written and actually finished. The first is Jim Levine, who called me one morning at seven A.M. after he heard one of my pieces on *Morning Edition* and said, "Have you ever thought of writing a book?" and I thought to myself, "Who *is* this guy?" Since then I have found out that he is a fascinating, astute man who is just plain smart as hell. I consider myself extremely lucky to be able to work with him and James Levine Communications.

Jim then sent me one of his agents, a bona fide genius as far as I'm concerned, to say nothing of a consummate hand-holder and girlfriend extraordinaire, Arielle Eckstut. Arielle tirelessly read every word of every draft, edited much of the initial pages, and was always there with words of encouragement at every turn. I accused her of having these phrases displayed on a flipchart near her phone for use with all of the insecure authors she has to work with. Things like, "Don't worry, *all* authors feel this way at first" and "You're doing great! How do you think Hemingway felt the first time around?" I will be forever in her debt and I consider her a girlfriend for life and, of course, you can't do much better than that.

To my editor, Mauro DiPreta at HarperCollins, I can only give an astonished thanks for displaying the perfect balance between encouraging me to "just write and see where it goes" and putting a gentle hand in when the manuscript was in desperate need of shaping and organization. He is also one of the funniest men I know, making him a riot to work with, and that is worth its weight in gold. Now that the book is finished, I miss his emails. It's almost enough to make me want to write another book. Not. And a thousand thanks to my production commandant, Anja Schmidt, one of the fastest women I've ever worked with, who guided this book from a sloppy manuscript to a bound product that sits on a shelf, with a cover and everything. I am thankful not only for her ability and speed, but for her good humor and unflagging support.

The fifth person is Mary Beth Kirchner. Simply put, much of my career would not have happened if it were not for her. I am resisting the impulse to wax on about it because she knows how deeply in her debt I will always be. Of course she is also a girlfriend for life.

And the last of these, but hardly the least, is my husband, Paul Goren. Paul was not only the most supportive man on earth and possibly the best natured (until he married me), but also never wavered in his confidence in me and in his willingness to do what he had to, to enable me to start, continue, and finish this project. And, perhaps most important, he never once objected to my batting him around the pages of this book, which I think is astonishing. So I am eternally grateful to him for his love, his support, and his ability to put up with me, to say nothing of the material he has provided me with over the years.

I also want to thank all of the people who unknowingly contributed to the book. First and foremost to all of my girlfriends who, over the years, have been—to quote myself— sustenance itself, without which life would be a vast pool of emptiness. They are, in alphabetical order: Barb Bentz, Betsy Bernadaud, Melissa Block, Lisa Brodkey, Cindy Carpien, Leslie Crary, Debby Dane, Marjorie Fedyszyn, Barb Freese, Beth Friend, Sarah Garber, Michelle Gazollo, Brooke Gladstone, Sally Greenwood, Lisa Gundersen, Bonnie Hoffman, Lisa Hsia, Janice Kaplan, Lucy Kaplansky, Jennifer Kaufman, Kathy Kirchner, Holly Kowitt, Danielle Matoon, Brigid McCarthy, Julia McEvoy, Sally Merar, Nora Moreno, Molly Murphy, Marge Ostroushko, Julie Osborn, Betsy Otto, Mary Ellen Page, Linda Paul, Julie Raskin, Francesca Rollins, Lori Rosenkrantz, Arlene Sagan, Betsy Sansby, Carrie Seid, Cecily Sommers, Stephanie Stone, Diana Wild, Peggy Wingo, Alice Winkler, Laura Ziegler, and Johanna Zorn.

To all my old boyfriends who were mean, oblivious, and insensitive, or rejected me in any way for any reason, I hope that you recognize yourself in these pages and are deeply humiliated in front of millions of readers.

A long time ago, a man named Bill Thomas allowed me on the air at WEFT-FM and essentially taught me much of what I know, literally overnight. Then, Ken Davis gave me a real job at WBEZ, where Johanna Zorn let me learn at her ankles. I still miss those days at WBEZ something fierce and all of the people I was lucky enough to work and play with: Nora Moreno, Karl Wright, Shel Lustig, Robbie Eiseman, Linda Paul, Neil Tesser, Claude Cunningham, Dorse Johnson, et al. When I moved to Washington, D.C., everything I knew got polished and refined through the saintly patience and good humor of people like John Tyler, who I will eternally adore, and I would give anything to work with him again. At NPR, I will always, always be indebted to Ira Glass, Sean Collins, Taki Telonidis, Brigid McCathy, Alice Winkler, Art Silverman, Brooke Gladstone, Bob Garfield, and Michael Sullivan—some of the best producers and editors you could ever work with. Any success I enjoy is to a great extent due to them.

I also want to express my deep appreciation to Rick Madden and the Corporation for Public Broadcasting for supporting my work over the years and being so incredibly patient and supportive.

Thanks to Sophia Levis, the inspired shortstop whose loyalty is unparalleled, and to Cece Lobin for having the brilliance to repeat the quintessentially female story as often as possible.

One day, a long time ago, a woman named Marion Usher turned to me and said, "Gwen, you're a writer!" Of course, I laughed in her face. I owe her an enormous debt that I can never repay, which, despite the fact that I laughed in her face, I hope she knows.

To the Gans family, all my love.

To my parents, John and Geraldine, and my siblings, Pam, Aaron, and Marian, an unspeakable thanks for simply . . . everything. Them I owe most of all.

And last, in memoriam to my uncle, Benjamin Gans, and my girlfriend, Lisa Dershin.